Percy Bysshe Shell   . He had his first schooling a   t twelve was sent to Eton.   College, Oxford, and about   his first book of verse appeared, *Original Poetry by Victor and Cazire*, written in part by his sister Elizabeth. After only five months Shelley, together with his friend Jefferson Hogg, was expelled from Oxford for publishing a pamphlet, 'The Necessity of Atheism'. This event marked the beginning of his estrangement from his family. In 1811 he eloped to Scotland with Harriet Westbrook, an innkeeper's daughter, and they were married in Edinburgh. For the next three years he and Harriet led a wandering life, and Shelley wrote scarcely any poetry apart from 'Queen Mab', concentrating instead on political prose works. A daughter, Ianthe, was born to them in 1813, but in the following year he and Harriet separated. Shortly afterwards Shelley left England with Mary Godwin, daughter of William Godwin, the philosopher with whom Shelley had been corresponding for some time. Harriet committed suicide in 1816. During the last years of his life, Shelley lived in Italy, that 'paradise of exiles' as he called it. He was drowned in 1822 in the Bay of Spezia, when his boat was caught by a sudden and violent storm on his return from a visit to Byron and Leigh Hunt at Pisa.

Shelley's life and personality have provoked endless interest and discussion. Southey wrote of him: 'With all his genius (and I think *most* highly of it), he was a base, bad man.' But Byron, in a reply to the publisher John Murray, who thought Shelley 'the vilest wretch now living', wrote: 'You were all brutally mistaken about Shelley, who was, without exception, the *best* and least selfish man I ever knew.'

Shelley

Poems

—◆—

Selected by Isabel Quigly

PENGUIN BOOKS

PENGUIN BOOKS

Published by the Penguin Group
Penguin Books Ltd, 27 Wrights Lane, London W8 5TZ, England
Penguin Books USA Inc., 375 Hudson Street, New York, New York 10014, USA
Penguin Books Australia Ltd, Ringwood, Victoria, Australia
Penguin Books Canada Ltd, 2801 John Street, Markham, Ontario, Canada L3R 1B4
Penguin Books (NZ) Ltd, 182–190 Wairau Road, Auckland 10, New Zealand

Penguin Books Ltd, Registered Offices: Harmondsworth, Middlesex, England

This selection first published 1956
7 9 10 8

Selection copyright © Penguin Books Ltd, 1956
All rights reserved

Printed in England by Clays Ltd, St Ives plc
Typeset in Monotype Bell

Except in the United States of America, this book is sold subject
to the condition that it shall not, by way of trade or otherwise, be lent,
re-sold, hired out, or otherwise circulated without the publisher's
prior consent in any form of binding or cover other than that in
which it is published and without a similar condition including this
condition being imposed on the subsequent purchaser

CONTENTS

5

CONTENTS

CONTENTS

INTRODUCTION

'WITH all his genius (and I think *most* highly of it),' Southey wrote of Shelley in 1830, 'he was a base, bad man.' 'Weak in genius,' Carlyle wrote of him, 'weak in character (for these two always go together); a poor, thin, spasmodic, hectic, shrill, and pallid being . . .' 'The vilest wretch now living,' John Murray, the publisher, called him. And even Lamb wrote: 'No one was ever the wiser or better for reading Shelley.'

In his lifetime or just after it Shelley aroused, as these opinions show, enormous personal virulence, and even to-day, more than a hundred and thirty years after his death, though his poetic reputation is secure, he can still raise temperatures and conjure violent antagonisms as a man. Probably more than any other English poet, more even than Byron, who cared immensely more for the effect he made, Shelley lives on outside his verse, and continues still to attract or repel, as he did when he was alive.

Those he repelled were generally, it is true, people who knew him only at second hand. His close friends were often his greatest admirers, and these included a number of tough and cynical men not at all in the habit of idealizing anyone. Byron, who was almost entirely uninclined, by nature and habit, for admiration, wrote to Murray: 'You were all brutally mistaken about Shelley, who was, without exception, the *best* and least selfish man I ever knew. I never knew anyone who was not a beast in comparison.' Edward Trelawney, the engaging Cornishman whose whole later life seemed to turn on the last months of his friendship with Shelley, wrote: 'To know an author personally is too often but to destroy the illusion created by his works . . . Shelley was a grand exception to this rule. To form a just idea of his poetry, you should have witnessed his daily life. . . The truth was, Shelley loved everything better than himself.' And Horace Smith called him by that now misused word 'gentleman', expanding it to 'gentle, generous, accomplished, brave'.

Between these two violently conflicting opinions – Murray's 'vilest' and Byron's emphatic '*best*' – it is no wonder that people are still, so many years after Shelley's death, confused about his personal merits. And, too, the romantic nineteenth-century portrait of him as a frail, large-eyed, and effeminate adolescent has done much to overlay the more robust account of him given by many who knew him, and to make one forget that at the time of his death he was close on thirty, a tall, stooping, but wiry man with greying hair, twice married, and the father of five children, who said a few days before he died: 'If I die tomorrow, I shall have lived to be older than my grandfather; I am ninety years old.'

Shelley was born in 1792, at Field Place, Warnham, in Sussex, and given the names of Percy Bysshe; the elder son of Mr Timothy Shelley, Member of Parliament and son of a rich and eccentric baronet, Sir Bysshe Shelley. His parents, though neither of them ill-natured, were neither of them particularly sympathetic to him. Of his mother he spoke little: she had been one of the beauties of the county, and, as she liked men of a sporting and military sort, her elder son was a disappointment to her; his father, a pompous, superficial, and rather stupid man, had liberal and even literary pretensions, but proved himself, in the face of Shelley, the personification of the outraged parent, and even after his son's death opposed the publication of his complete works with extraordinary persistence.

Shelley got his first lessons from a local clergyman, his first schooling at Sion House Academy at Isleworth, and at twelve was sent to Eton, in those days, under the rule of the ferocious Dr Keate, a freer and far tougher place than it is today. The stories of his Eton days have become a part of the Shelley legend: how he refused to fag, was known as 'mad Shelley', was the victim of organized 'Shelley-hunts', and, under the spell of the terror novels of Monk Lewis and Mrs Radcliffe, became an amateur alchemist, devil-raiser, and novelist – with a published novel, *Zastrozzi*, to his credit before he left school. Mrs Shelley, in her notes to 'Queen Mab', set the tone for future biographers when she wrote: 'Inspired with ardour for the acquisition of knowledge, endowed with the keenest sensibility and with the fortitude of a martyr, Shelley came among his fellow-creatures, congregated for the purposes of education, like a spirit from another sphere; too delicately organized for the rough treatment man uses towards man, especially in the season of youth, and too resolute in carrying out his own sense of good and justice, not to become a victim.' All of it true, no doubt, but as a description of a twelve-year-old boy's arrival at school rather likely to raise a smile.

When he was just eighteen he went up to University College, Oxford, installed there by his father, who gave him unlimited credit for books and stationery. About the same time his first book of verse, *Original Poetry by Victor and Cazire*, written in part by his sister Elizabeth, appeared; several of Shelley's contributions were addressed to his cousin, Harriet Grove, with whom he was then in love. At Oxford he became friendly with another undergraduate, Jefferson Hogg, who was the first of a series of rather hard-headed, practical, and worldly friends whom Shelley attracted, probably by the complete dissimilarity of his nature and theirs; and after only five months at the university the pair of them were expelled for issuing a pamphlet entitled *The Necessity of Atheism*.

This abrupt end to his university career was the beginning of Shelley's estrangement from his family, and the financial and other difficulties in which it placed him. But he was never – except for a very short period – in desperate need of money. During the rest of his life, and particularly after his grandfather's death early in 1815, he had an income, small but assured, and expectations of a large fortune, on which he was able to obtain advances. Financial worries were the least of his troubles, and what he had of them were due chiefly to his extreme generosity to his friends, and even to a number of dependants who, like William Godwin, had long ceased to be his friends.

Shelley and Hogg went to London, efforts were made, successfully, to separate them, and in August of the same year (1811) Shelley, then barely nineteen, eloped to Scotland with a schoolgirl of seventeen, an innkeeper's daughter called Harriet Westbrook, and married her in Edinburgh, where shortly afterwards they were joined by Hogg. For the next three years, during which Shelley wrote scarcely any poetry except 'Queen Mab', but a number of political prose works, he and Harriet led a wandering life. A daughter, Ianthe, was born to them in 1813, and in March of the following year Shelley remarried Harriet with a Church of England ceremony, since he was not certain of the legality of his Scottish marriage and probably feared for the legitimacy of his children. Two months later, however, he and Harriet separated; and in the following July Shelley left England for the Continent with Mary Godwin, daughter of William Godwin the philosopher, with whom Shelley had been corresponding for two years. With them, as interpreter, went Mary's half-sister, Claire Claremont. Again after two months they returned to England, and shortly afterwards, in November, Harriet gave birth to her second child, Charles Bysshe.

Shelley's relations with women have been very fully discussed by his biographers, and probably caused more prejudice against him, both during his lifetime and after it, than any of his anti-religious – which in fact meant anti-clerical – opinions. Whatever one may feel about the *fact* of his desertion of Harriet, and her suicide two years later by drowning in the Serpentine, it is as well to remember that he was eighteen when he came to know her, that he married her partly for chivalrous reasons, being persuaded that she was persecuted and unhappy at her school; and that his affection for her was from the first confused with pity for her position and, knowing as he did that she loved him, with a feeling of responsibility for her happiness.

Mary Godwin must have appeared to him to have the qualities he had missed in Harriet: a background he could admire (Godwin for a father, Mary Wollstonecraft, author of *The Rights of Women*, for a mother), a seriousness and ardour, a certain weight of personality, and the intellectual ambitions Harriet lacked.

In fact, however, she too proved very far from the ideal companion for whom Shelley was always searching: a heavy, pretentious person (Byron found her vulgar), her single virtue in relation to Shelley consisted in the fact that, for all his waywardness, she never ceased to love him. His relations with a number of other women – among them Claire Claremont, who was frequently one of their household, and the mother of Byron's child Allegra, Jane Williams, whose lover Edward Williams was drowned with Shelley, and to whom his last poems are addressed, or even Emilia Viviani, for whom the most magnificent of all his love poems, 'Epipsychidion', was written – are hard to establish exactly. Shelley was extremely attractive to women, for his very idealism – and also for a certain inability to see what went on under his nose – extremely unperceptive of the ordinary ways in which people behave, and, in his search for an intellectual 'sister of his soul', very often entirely unaware, it seems, of where his own feelings or those of the woman concerned were leading them. There was, through all Shelley's life, a kind of innocence of heart about him that was easily sneered at by his detractors, but recognized for what it was by his friends and even by the woman who suffered most from it – Mary herself.

The rest of Shelley's life – a little over seven years – was spent in moving from place to place, mostly on the Continent, and, during the last few years of it, in Italy, that 'paradise of exiles', as he called it. Three children were born to him and Mary, of whom only the youngest, Percy Florence, survived, and later inherited the baronetcy; the other two, William and Clara, died as very small children in Italy. Among Shelley's friends were Hogg (though the friendship fluctuated), Leigh Hunt, Trelawney, who later – though he was incapable of sticking to the literal truth about anything – wrote extensively and entertainingly about Shelley and Byron, Byron (though Shelley's feeling for him had cooled considerably by the time of his death), and, perhaps the man he was most attached to when he died, Edward Williams, with whom he used to go sailing.

During the last weeks of his life the Shelleys, Jane and Edward Williams, and for part of the time Claire Claremont were all sharing the Casa Magni near Portovenere on the Gulf of Spezia: a very beautiful part of the coast, but subject to storms of great suddenness and violence. One of these caught the boat *Don Juan*, which Shelley had renamed the *Ariel*, when he, with Edward Williams and a boy for crew, was returning in it from a visit to Byron and Hunt at Pisa. The bodies were missing for ten days; and Shelley's was cast ashore near Viareggio on 18 July, 1822, recognizable only from the clothes and a volume of

Aeschylus in one of the pockets. In the following month Byron, Hunt, and Trelawney burned the body on the beach at Viareggio, and the ashes were taken to the Protestant Cemetery in Rome, of which Shelley had written : 'It might make one in love with death, to think that one should be buried in so sweet a place.'

For all the contradictory reports about him, Shelley was a consistent though not a simple person, and it is necessary, in considering him, to differentiate between the extravagant romanticism of the schoolboy, and the mature, not quite disillusioned but oddly unexpectant Shelley of 1822. The devil-conjuring, wild-haired schoolboy remained, to some extent, in the adult Shelley, but there was an immense difference, and one not only of personality, between the boy who attributed all the evils of the world to tyranny, and felt that by altering the circumstances of the world these evils would vanish, and the man who found the conflict of good and evil – as of freedom and oppression – in the nature of man himself. Ardour, idealism, generosity, and the more attractive qualities of youth he had almost to excess, but with the intellectual long-sightedness that often goes with them, and a lack of self-criticism, both moral and poetic, that came near, at times, to self-dramatization. The image of the frail, pure, and noble poet, reviled by the world, is a familiar one in his verse; but, for all that he came near to saying so, there was about Shelley a nobility of spirit, a height of purpose, a kind of fine-grainedness that is a quality of birth and cannot be grown to. The shrillness and febrility often attributed to him is really a matter of personality; for, whatever people think of his character, there will always be those who dislike the particular type of personality of which Shelley was so outstanding – one might almost say excessive – an example : passionate, highly strung, vocal, and of an extreme delicacy of looks. Shelley's fairness, the etherial, mermanlike quality of his appearance, his fragility and sweetness, have all been overstressed. That he had all these qualities is true, but they were balanced by a strength of personality that made him, apparently, unforgettable. No good portrait exists of him, and what portraits there are have mostly exaggerated the romantic qualities of frailness and grace. Even the descriptions of him given by his friends tend to heighten the quality each man looked for in him. Trelawney exaggerates the girlishness, the shyness, the fey quality he found so puzzling and attractive in Shelley, Hogg looks at him with a certain irony, fond but a bit backhanded, and Peacock seems to have in mind an amusing and satirically-viewed Shelley – the delightful but hardly literal and solid Scythrop of *Nightmare Abbey*. Later writers have stressed the 'angelic' aspect, and Matthew Arnold's phrase 'a beautiful and ineffectual angel' has stuck where other, and more profound, judgements have been forgotten.

Shelley's poetic personality, if one may call it so, was closely akin to his personality as a man. He lacked what Keats called 'negative capability', the ability to enter into the being even of inanimate things for the purposes of poetry, and to lose a literal nature in that of the artist. He was never – it did not enter his head to be so – a 'pure' artist in the sense that Keats was one : hence the diffusion of his poetic energies that Keats complained of in him, even the technical scattering of his powers that gave Keats the impression of a certain thinness of texture in his verse. Shelley is nearly always obtrusive in his verse. Even where he is technically happiest you seldom forget his presence : not only because he deliberately treated themes which were near his heart (the overthrowing of tyranny, and so on), introduced himself in some thin disguise very often, or wrote wholly personal love lyrics, but because he managed always, through the repetition of certain images, the association of certain colours, a certain texture in his language, to conjure an entirely Shelleyan world: cloudy and radiant at once, remote but imaginatively credible.

To his contemporaries this world – and Shelley's verse in general – appeared, as the work of new poets often does, turgid and obscure. From this distance it is easy for us to see Shelley in the middle of a neat literary period that began with the publication of the *Lyrical Ballads* of Wordsworth in 1798, and ended with the death of Byron in 1824. But to his contemporaries things were far less clear-cut. It was an age, like ours, of violent transition, social and intellectual, in which the old ways of thought, in religion, in morals, in behaviour, and in art – a whole outlook and a way of life – were being questioned. The French Revolution had blown the eighteenth-century world sky-high, and, more gradually but no less effectively, the Industrial Revolution in England was transforming the face of the countryside and the way of life of its people. In all this turmoil it was not likely that poets, who tend to be in the vanguard of opinion, would sit quietly. A revolution in poetry had, indeed, been brewing from the middle of the eighteenth century, and Gray, Collins, Cowper, and others had all gone a certain way in the Romantic direction. The poetical conventions among which they found themselves derived directly from Pope and Dryden: Dryden who made of the heroic couplet, and of worldly, politically-flavoured, satirically-treated verse, a thing of immense vigour, variety, and power, and Pope who raised that type of verse to a subtlety and delicacy none of his followers could achieve. Both Pope and Dryden were – paradoxical as it may sound – passionate writers, not only passionately interested in the technique of verse writing, but with strong feelings on the subjects they treated; but their successors, lacking both their gifts and their intensity, brought poetry down to what Wordsworth called 'triviality and meanness, both of thought and language'.

It took a major poet, not merely to break with the past, but to establish canons for the future. And this Wordsworth, in the *Lyrical Ballads*, set out very deliberately to do. In his famous Preface to the second edition, he plainly put down his beliefs and objects in relation to poetry. 'All good poetry', he wrote, 'is the spontaneous overflow of powerful feelings.' To us, brought up at the tail end of the Romantic movement, this does not seem a revolutionary statement; but to anyone taught in a more classical school the idea of poetry 'overflowing', the very notion of spontaneity as a virtue, must have appeared astonishing.

Shelley grew up in these aesthetic controversies, and his reading was largely among those who were then the moderns. 'Our earlier English poetry', wrote Mrs Shelley, 'was almost unknown to him. The love and knowledge of nature developed by Wordsworth – the lofty melody and mysterious beauty of Coleridge's poetry – and the wild fantastic scenery adopted by Southey – composed his favourite reading.' He was no innovator in an eighteenth-century world, as Wordsworth and Coleridge had been; the Romantic climate was by his time established. But he was, in spirit, the most essentially romantic of the poets of his age, and his faults were all faults of an overabundant and undisciplined imagination. No poet better repays cutting; no great poet was ever less worth reading in his entirety. He lacked almost entirely a dramatic sense, though he did not realize it (it is interesting to know that he disliked the theatre); he had no ability for satire, and his humorous verse is generally so bad that it is embarrassing to read. Technically he was brilliant but erratic, and his very facility in writing was at times disastrous, for, coupled with his inability to criticize himself, it made him often careless, repetitive, and lazy in his choice of words.

But his great gift – and he had it supremely – was as a lyric poet. Even his long poems are at their best sustained lyrics, and, for all his belief in the moral and, when he was very young, the propagandist power of verse, for all his large claim that 'poets are the unacknowledged legislators of the world', it was the lyrical content of poetry that in practice chiefly interested him. 'A poet is a nightingale', he wrote in *A Defence of Poetry*, 'who sits in darkness and sings to cheer its own solitude with sweet sounds.' And this very often is just what Shelley appears to be doing. It is easier, very often, to follow his verse aurally, than to track down intellectually where his images are leading; whether this is a good or a bad thing poetically (and it depends what you are looking for in poetry), the literal meaning of the words often gets lost in the musical qualities of the language. Stephen Spender has called Shelley's 'Ode to the West Wind' 'the most symphonic poem in the English language', and numerous other musical analogies could be made with other poems of his. It is ironical that Shelley, who so firmly believed in his philosophical, moral, and social responsibilities, should be remembered chiefly for something quite distinct from them; but it is also true that, as he grew older, Shelley came to look on his poetry less and less as a moral mouthpiece.

For all this, much of his verse – and not all of it bad verse – is didactic: 'Queen Mab', for instance, his first important poem, an odd mixture of fantasy, fairytale, and political theory; 'The Revolt of Islam', his second long – indeed overlong – poem (if 'Alastor' counts as short); and, at his greatest and still didactic, 'Prometheus Unbound', a drama on so heroic a scale that his lack of dramatic competence does not matter, for this is not theatre but huge metaphysical grand-opera, where the scenery can creak if the singing is good enough.

Autobiography, too, appealed naturally to Shelley, and while his short lyrics give personal clues to his state of mind at a particular moment and in relation to a particular woman, it is in the longer 'Alastor' that you find a full-length portrait, idealized but unmistakable:

> The brave, the gentle, and the beautiful,
> The child of grace and genius.

The same figure appears, more personally acknowledged, and with deeper marks of suffering, in 'Adonais'; this time it is:

> A pardlike Spirit beautiful and swift –
> A Love in desolation masked; – a Power
> Girt round with weakness.

And in the 'Ode to the West Wind' he becomes 'tameless and swift and proud'. But this is portraiture, and static. For a record of Shelley's spiritual development there is 'Epipsychidion', where, with an intensity he never equalled, even in the shorter lyrics, he described the progress of his search for the ideal, and his whole conception of love. Whatever he felt for the literal woman to whom the poem is addressed, Emilia Viviani (and it is ironical that soon after it was written she was bothering him for money: 'so much', said Mary, with understandable tartness, 'for Percy's platonics'), she was the excuse for an 'absolute' emotion, one which, in human terms, could not humanly progress; and so the poem ends with a kind of oblivion, physical and spiritual, in the lover, as if he had reached, in his final circle of experience, an unsustainable pitch.

The shorter lyrics want reading, not expounding; and

even the stateliest of them (longer, but still lyrical),
'Adonais', is self-explanatory. It has been criticized as cold;
'monumental' is the favourite adjective. But Shelley was
writing on a subject for which he felt a deep, but not an
intimate, sympathy, and there is all the difference between
the loss of a valued but slightly known contemporary –
which is what Keats was to him – and the death of a close
friend. Technically perhaps the most flawless of his poems,
'Adonais' is, for what it sets out to be – not, that is, a
personal outburst but an elegy, somewhat in the tradition
of 'Lycidas' (in which Milton, too, was not mourning the
death of a close friend) – entirely successful, and – I at
any rate find – among the most moving of his poems, as
well as the most beautiful.

As 'Adonais' superbly shows, Shelley varied, in mood as
in style; and it is a pity to look on the world conjured by
the imagery of, say, his best-known lyric, 'Swiftly walk
over the western wave, Spirit of Night', as the only one
in which he could live imaginatively. There is the crisp,
brilliantly visual imagery that conjures a wholly Mediter-
ranean climate, of the 'Lines Written among the Euganean
Hills'; the charming, modest world of quite pedestrian
pleasures in the 'Letter to Maria Gisborne'; the tender
almost-sophistication of his final poems to Jane Williams,
in which he has grown more to sprite than to lover, and
finds the position of Ariel preferable to that of a more con-
ventional Ferdinand; the long horror of 'The Cenci', and
the (for Shelley) curiously restrained beauty at the end;
the fiery lightness of 'The Cloud'; the for once effective
indignation in that flaming sonnet on England in 1819 that
starts 'An old, mad, blind, despised, and dying king'.

Shelley had width as well as intensity, not only of subject
but of style; a greater range of experience and of mood
than he is often credited with, since his nature was

rounder, subtler, and far more interesting than is often supposed. If one must grade poets he comes, in the hierarchy of his period, well after Wordsworth and Keats. In what was, after the Elizabethan, the richest age poetically in England, that is not a poor position. And Shelley is one of the few poets who, being little subject to changes of fashion in poetic taste, needs no poetic championing. He is his own best defender, in the best – but only the best – of his unequal poetry.

ISABEL QUIGLY

MAIN DATES IN THE LIFE OF SHELLEY

1792 Born 4 August at Field Place, Warnham, Sussex, elder
son of Mr Timothy Shelley, M.P.

1802 Sion House Academy, Isleworth.

1804 Eton College.

1810 *Zastrozzi* (a novel) published.
Original Poetry by Victor and Cazire (by Shelley and
his sister Elizabeth) published.
University College, Oxford; meets Thomas Jefferson
Hogg.
Posthumous Fragments of Margaret Nicholson (by
Shelley and Hogg) and *St Irvyne* published.

1811 *Necessity of Atheism* (pamphlet by Shelley and Hogg)
issued; both expelled.
London with Hogg; Radnorshire.
Elopes to Edinburgh with Harriet Westbrook; mar-
ries her there.
York; Keswick; meets Southey.

1812 Begins to correspond with William Godwin; Dublin;
Wales; meets Peacock; Lynmouth; 'Queen Mab'
begun; Wales; London and meets Godwin; Wales
again.

1813 Wales; Ireland; London.
Ianthe, a daughter, born to Harriet.
Lake District; Edinburgh; Windsor.

1814 Marries Harriet with Church of England ceremony.
In May Harriet leaves him.
In July leaves for the Continent with Mary Woll-
stonecraft Godwin, daughter of William Godwin,
accompanied by Jane (Claire) Claremont.
France; Switzerland; the Netherlands.
London in September, penniless.
Charles Bysshe born to Harriet

1815 Sir Bysshe Shelley, Shelley's grandfather, dies; financial
      settlement with his father.
      Devon; Windsor.
      'Alastor'; 'Essay on Christianity'.

1816 William born to Mary.
      Geneva with Mary, William, and Claire; meets
      Byron.
      'Mont Blanc'; 'Hymn to Intellectual Beauty'.
      England again, Bath.
      Harriet commits suicide.
      Marries Mary.

1817 Children by Harriet placed under guardianship by
      Chancery court.
      'Revolt of Islam'; 'Prince Athanase'.
      Clara born to Mary.

1818 Italy with Mary, Claire, and the two children.
      Lucca.
      'Rosalind and Helen'; *Symposium* translated.
      Venice.
      'Lines written among the Euganean Hills'.
      Clara dies.
      'Julian and Maddalo'; *Prometheus Unbound* begun.
      Rome; Naples.

1819 Rome.
      Acts II and III of *Prometheus Unbound*.
      The Cenci.
      William dies.
      Leghorn; Florence; Rome.
      'Mask of Anarchy'; 'Ode to the West Wind';
      'Cyclops'; 'Peter Bell the Third'.
      Percy Florence born to Mary.
      Act IV of *Prometheus Unbound*.

1820 Pisa; Leghorn; San Giuliano, near Pisa.
      Meets Emilia Viviani.

1821 'Epipsychidion'; *Defence of Poetry*.
Lerici; San Giuliano.
Meets Edward and Jane Williams.
'Adonais'.
Ravenna.

1822 Meets Trelawney.
Charles I.
San Terenzo, near Portovenere.
8 July : Drowned near La Spezia.
18 July : Body cast ashore near Viareggio.
16 August : Body burnt on the beach at Viareggio by Byron, Hunt, and Trelawney.
7 December : Ashes buried in the Protestant Cemetery, Rome.

TEXTUAL NOTE

THE task of any editor of Shelley is complicated by the poet's eccentricities of spelling and punctuation, by his carelessness both in transcribing and in correcting the proofs of his poems, and by the fact that many poems were printed without his seeing them through the press himself and many more appeared only after his death, taken from notebooks and manuscripts that were indescribably confused. The text used in this selection of Shelley's poems is that of the Oxford edition, edited by Thomas Hutchinson in 1904 as the result of a scholarly collating of the early texts and editions, with acknowledgement to the work of such former editors as Richard Garnett and H. Buxton Forman. Hutchinson revised a good deal of the original punctuation – as indeed every editor of Shelley is bound to do – and some of the original spelling; but in certain words, such as *aëry*, where the spelling was peculiarly and consistently Shelley's own, he retained the original. In this selection the many variant readings of particular lines and phrases are not given, and those who are interested in them should consult a complete edition of the poems.

In this edition the poems are printed in the order in which they were written, as far as it is known.

QUEEN MAB

I

How wonderful is Death,
　Death and his brother Sleep!
One, pale as yonder waning moon
　With lips of lurid blue;
The other, rosy as the morn
　When throned on ocean's wave
　It blushes o'er the world:
Yet both so passing wonderful!

Hath then the gloomy Power
Whose reign is in the tainted sepulchres
　Seized on her sinless soul?
　Must then that peerless form
Which love and admiration cannot view
Without a beating heart, those azure veins
Which steal like streams along a field of snow,
　That lovely outline, which is fair
　As breathing marble, perish?
　Must putrefaction's breath
　Leave nothing of this heavenly sight
　But loathsomeness and ruin?
Spare nothing but a gloomy theme,
On which the lightest heart might moralize?
Or is it only a sweet slumber
　Stealing o'er sensation,
Which the breath of roseate morning
　Chaseth into darkness?
　Will Ianthe wake again,
And give that faithful bosom joy

Whose sleepless spirit waits to catch
Light, life and rapture from her smile?

Yes! she will wake again,
Although her glowing limbs are motionless,
And silent those sweet lips,
Once breathing eloquence,
That might have soothed a tiger's rage,
Or thawed the cold heart of a conqueror.
Her dewy eyes are closed,
And on their lids, whose texture fine
Scarce hides the dark blue orbs beneath,
The baby Sleep is pillowed:
Her golden tresses shade
The bosom's stainless pride,
Curling like tendrils of the parasite
Around a marble column.

Hark! whence that rushing sound?
'Tis like the wondrous strain
That round a lonely ruin swells,
Which, wandering on the echoing shore,
The enthusiast hears at evening:
'Tis softer than the west wind's sigh;
'Tis wilder than the unmeasured notes
Of that strange lyre whose strings
The genii of the breezes sweep:
Those lines of rainbow light
Are like the moonbeams when they fall
Through some cathedral window, but the tints
Are such as may not find
Comparison on earth.

Behold the chariot of the Fairy Queen!
Celestial coursers paw the unyielding air;
Their filmy pennons at her word they furl,
And stop obedient to the reins of light:
  These the Queen of Spells drew in,
   She spread a charm around the spot,
And leaning graceful from the aethereal car,
  Long did she gaze, and silently,
    Upon the slumbering maid.

Oh! not the visioned poet in his dreams,
When silvery clouds float through the 'wildered
    brain,
When every sight of lovely, wild and grand
  Astonishes, enraptures, elevates,
   When fancy at a glance combines
   The wondrous and the beautiful, –
  So bright, so fair, so wild a shape
   Hath ever yet beheld,
As that which reined the coursers of the air,
  And poured the magic of her gaze
   Upon the maiden's sleep.

  The broad and yellow moon
   Shone dimly through her form –
That form of faultless symmetry;
The pearly and pellucid car
  Moved not the moonlight's line:
  'Twas not an earthly pageant:
Those who had looked upon the sight,
  Passing all human glory,
  Saw not the yellow moon,
  Saw not the mortal scene,
  Heard not the night-wind's rush,

Heard not an earthly sound,
Saw but the fairy pageant,
Heard but the heavenly strains
That filled the lonely dwelling.

The Fairy's frame was slight, yon fibrous cloud,
That catches but the palest tinge of even,
And which the straining eye can hardly seize
When melting into eastern twilight's shadow,
Were scarce so thin, so slight; but the fair star
That gems the glittering coronet of morn,
Sheds not a light so mild, so powerful,
As that which, bursting from the Fairy's form,
Spread a purpureal halo round the scene,
Yet with an undulating motion,
Swayed to her outline gracefully.

From her celestial car
The Fairy Queen descended,
And thrice she waved her wand
Circled with wreaths of amaranth:
Her thin and misty form
Moved with the moving air,
And the clear silver tones,
As thus she spoke, were such
As are unheard by all but gifted ear.

11

IF solitude hath ever led thy steps
To the wild Ocean's echoing shore,
And thou hast lingered there,
Until the sun's broad orb
Seemed resting on the burnished wave,

Thou must have marked the lines
Of purple gold, that motionless
　　Hung o'er the sinking sphere:
Thou must have marked the billowy clouds
Edged with intolerable radiancy
　　Towering like rocks of jet
　　Crowned with a diamond wreath.
　　And yet there is a moment,
　　When the sun's highest point
Peeps like a star o'er Ocean's western edge,
When those far clouds of feathery gold,
　Shaded with deepest purple, gleam
　Like islands on a dark blue sea;
Then has thy fancy soared above the earth,
　　And furled its wearied wing
　　Within the Fairy's fane.

　　Yet not the golden islands
　　Gleaming in yon flood of light,
　　　Nor the feathery curtains
　　Stretching o'er the sun's bright couch,
　　Nor the burnished Ocean waves
　　Paving that gorgeous dome,
　So fair, so wonderful a sight
As Mab's aethereal palace could afford.
Yet likest evening's vault, that faery Hall!
As Heaven, low resting on the wave, it spread
　　Its floors of flashing light,
　　Its vast and azure dome,
　　Its fertile golden islands
　　Floating on a silver sea;
Whilst suns their mingling beamings darted
Through clouds of circumambient darkness,

And pearly battlements around
Looked o'er the immense of Heaven.

FROM VI

'Throughout these infinite orbs of mingling light,
Of which yon earth is one, is wide diffused
A Spirit of activity and life,
That knows no term, cessation, or decay;
That fades not when the lamp of earthly life,
Extinguished in the dampness of the grave,
Awhile there slumbers, more than when the babe
In the dim newness of its being feels
The impulses of sublunary things,
And all is wonder to unpractised sense:
But, active, steadfast, and eternal, still
Guides the fierce whirlwind, in the tempest roars,
Cheers in the day, breathes in the balmy groves,
Strengthens in health, and poisons in disease;
And in the storm of change, that ceaselessly
Rolls round the eternal universe, and shakes
Its undecaying battlement, presides,
Apportioning with irresistible law
The place each spring of its machine shall fill;
So that when waves on waves tumultuous heap
Confusion to the clouds, and fiercely driven
Heaven's lightnings scorch the uprooted ocean-
    fords,
Whilst, to the eye of shipwrecked mariner,
Lone sitting on the bare and shuddering rock,
All seems unlinked contingency and chance:
No atom of this turbulence fulfils
A vague and unnecessitated task,
Or acts but as it must and ought to act.

Even the minutest molecule of light,
That in an April sunbeam's fleeting glow
Fulfils its destined, though invisible work,
The universal Spirit guides; nor less,
When merciless ambition, or mad zeal,
Has led two hosts of dupes to battlefield,
That, blind, they there may dig each other's graves,
And call the sad work glory, does it rule
All passions: not a thought, a will, an act,
No working of the tyrant's moody mind,
Nor one misgiving of the slaves who boast
Their servitude, to hide the shame they feel,
Nor the events enchaining every will,
That from the depths of unrecorded time
Have drawn all-influencing virtue, pass
Unrecognized, or unforeseen by thee,
Soul of the Universe! eternal spring
Of life and death, of happiness and woe,
Of all that chequers the phantasmal scene
That floats before our eyes in wavering light,
Which gleams but on the darkness of our prison,
　　Whose chains and massy walls
　　We feel, but cannot see.

'Spirit of Nature! all-sufficing Power,
Necessity! thou mother of the world!
Unlike the God of human error, thou
Requir'st no prayers or praises; the caprice
Of man's weak will belongs no more to thee
Than do the changeful passions of his breast
To thy unvarying harmony: the slave,
Whose horrible lusts spread misery o'er the world,
And the good man, who lifts, with virtuous pride,
His being, in the sight of happiness,

That springs from his own works; the poison-tree,
Beneath whose shade all life is withered up,
And the fair oak, whose leafy dome affords
A temple where the vows of happy love
Are registered, are equal in thy sight:
No love, no hate thou cherishest; revenge
And favouritism, and worst desire of fame
Thou know'st not: all that the wide world contains
Are but thy passive instruments, and thou
Regard'st them all with an impartial eye,
Whose joy or pain thy nature cannot feel,
   Because thou hast not human sense,
   Because thou art not human mind.'

STANZA, WRITTEN AT BRACKNELL

THY dewy looks sink in my breast;
  Thy gentle words stir poison there;
Thou hast disturbed the only rest
  That was the portion of despair!
Subdued to Duty's hard control,
  I could have borne my wayward lot:
The chains that bind this ruined soul
  Had cankered then – but crushed it not.

STANZAS–APRIL 1814

Away! the moor is dark beneath the moon,
  Rapid clouds have drank the last pale beam of even:
Away! the gathering winds will call the darkness soon,
  And profoundest midnight shroud the serene lights of
    heaven.

Pause not! The time is past! Every voice cries, Away!
  Tempt not with one last tear thy friend's ungentle mood:
Thy lover's eye, so glazed and cold, dares not entreat thy
    stay:
  Duty and dereliction guide thee back to solitude.

Away, away! to thy sad and silent home;
  Pour bitter tears on its desolated hearth;
Watch the dim shades as like ghosts they go and come,
  And complicate strange webs of melancholy mirth.

The leaves of wasted autumn woods shall float around thine
    head:
  The blooms of dewy spring shall gleam beneath thy feet:
But thy soul or this world must fade in the frost that binds
    the dead,
  Ere midnight's frown and morning's smile, ere thou and
    peace may meet.

The cloud shadows of midnight possess their own repose,
  For the weary winds are silent, or the moon is in the deep:
Some respite to its turbulence unresting ocean knows;
  Whatever moves, or toils, or grieves, hath its appointed
    sleep.

Thou in the grave shalt rest — yet till the phantoms flee
  Which that house and heath and garden made dear to thee
    erewhile,
Thy remembrance, and repentance, and deep musings are
  not free
  From the music of two voices and the light of one sweet
    smile.

TO HARRIET

THY look of love has power to calm
　　The stormiest passion of my soul;
Thy gentle words are drops of balm
　　In life's too bitter bowl;
No grief is mine, but that alone
These choicest blessings I have known.

Harriet! if all who long to live
　　In the warm sunshine of thine eye,
That price beyond all pain must give, –
　　Beneath thy scorn to die;
Then hear thy chosen own too late
His heart most worthy of thy hate.

Be thou, then, one among mankind
　　Whose heart is harder not for state,
Thou only virtuous, gentle, kind,
　　Amid a world of hate;
And by a slight endurance seal
A fellow-being's lasting weal.

For pale with anguish is his cheek,
　　His breath comes fast, his eyes are dim,
Thy name is struggling ere he speak,
　　Weak is each trembling limb;
In mercy let him not endure
The misery of a fatal cure.

Oh, trust for once no erring guide!
　　Bid the remorseless feeling flee;
'Tis malice, 'tis revenge, 'tis pride,
　　'Tis anything but thee;
Oh, deign a nobler pride to prove,
And pity if thou canst not love.

TO MARY WOLLSTONECRAFT GODWIN

I

Mine eyes were dim with tears unshed;
   Yes, I was firm – thus wert not thou;–
My baffled looks did fear yet dread
   To meet thy looks – I could not know
How anxiously they sought to shine
With soothing pity upon mine.

II

To sit and curb the soul's mute rage
   Which preys upon itself alone;
To curse the life which is the cage
   Of fettered grief that dares not groan,
Hiding from many a careless eye
The scornèd load of agony.

III

Whilst thou alone, then not regarded,
   The   thou alone should be,
To spend years thus, and be rewarded,
   As thou, sweet love, requited me
When none were near – Oh! I did wake
From torture for that moment's sake.

IV

Upon my heart thy accents sweet
   Of peace and pity fell like dew
On flowers half dead; – thy lips did meet
   Mine tremblingly; thy dark eyes threw
Their soft persuasion on my brain,
Charming away its dream of pain.

V

We are not happy, sweet! our state
    Is strange and full of doubt and fear;
More need of words that ills abate; —
    Reserve or censure come not near
Our sacred friendship, lest there be
No solace left for thee and me.

MUTABILITY

WE are as clouds that veil the midnight moon;
   How restlessly they speed, and gleam, and quiver,
Streaking the darkness radiantly! – yet soon
   Night closes round, and they are lost for ever:

Or like forgotten lyres, whose dissonant strings
   Give various response to each varying blast,
To whose frail frame no second motion brings
   One mood or modulation like the last.

We rest. – A dream has power to poison sleep;
   We rise. – One wandering thought pollutes the day;
We feel, conceive or reason, laugh or weep;
   Embrace fond woe, or cast our cares away:

It is the same! – For, be it joy or sorrow,
   The path of its departure still is free:
Man's yesterday may ne'er be like his morrow;
   Nought may endure but Mutability.

ON DEATH

THE pale, the cold, and the moony smile
  Which the meteor beam of a starless night
Sheds on a lonely and sea-girt isle,
  Ere the dawning of morn's undoubted light,
Is the flame of life so fickle and wan
That flits round our steps till their strength is gone.

O man! hold thee on in courage of soul
  Through the stormy shades of thy worldly way,
And the billows of cloud that around thee roll
  Shall sleep in the light of a wondrous day,
Where Hell and Heaven shall leave thee free
To the universe of destiny.

This world is the nurse of all we know,
  This world is the mother of all we feel,
And the coming of death is a fearful blow
  To a brain unencompassed with nerves of steel;
When all that we know, or feel, or see,
Shall pass like an unreal mystery.

The secret things of the grave are there,
  Where all but this frame must surely be,
Though the fine-wrought eye and the wondrous ear
  No longer will live to hear or to see
All that is great and all that is strange
In the boundless realm of unending change.

Who telleth a tale of unspeaking death?
  Who lifteth the veil of what is to come?
Who painteth the shadows that are beneath
  The wide-winding caves of the peopled tomb?
Or uniteth the hopes of what shall be
With the fears and the love for that which we see?

TO —

Oh! there are spirits of the air,
  And genii of the evening breeze,
And gentle ghosts, with eyes as fair
  As star-beams among twilight trees: –
Such lovely ministers to meet
Oft hast thou turned from men thy lonely feet.

With mountain winds, and babbling springs,
  And moonlight seas, that are the voice
Of these inexplicable things,
  Thou didst hold commune, and rejoice
When they did answer thee; but they
Cast, like a worthless boon, thy love away.

And thou hast sought in starry eyes
  Beams that were never meant for thine,
Another's wealth: – tame sacrifice
  To a fond faith! still dost thou pine?
Still dost thou hope that greeting hands,
Voice, looks, or lips, may answer thy demands?

Ah! wherefore didst thou build thine hope
  On the false earth's inconstancy?
Did thine own mind afford no scope
  Of love, or moving thoughts to thee?
That natural scenes or human smiles
Could steal the power to wind thee in their wiles?

Yes, all the faithless smiles are fled
  Whose falsehood left thee broken-hearted;
The glory of the moon is dead;
  Night's ghosts and dreams have now departed;
Thine own soul still is true to thee,
But changed to a foul fiend through misery.

This fiend, whose ghastly presence ever
   Beside thee like thy shadow hangs,
Dream not to chase; – the mad endeavour
   Would scourge thee to severer pangs.
Be as thou art. Thy settled fate,
Dark as it is, all change would aggravate.

TO WORDSWORTH

Poet of Nature, thou hast wept to know
That things depart which never may return:
Childhood and youth, friendship and love's first glow,
Have fled like sweet dreams, leaving thee to mourn.
These common woes I feel. One loss is mine
Which thou too feel'st, yet I alone deplore.
Thou wert as a lone star, whose light did shine
On some frail bark in winter's midnight roar:
Thou hast like to a rock-built refuge stood
Above the blind and battling multitude:
In honoured poverty thy voice did weave
Songs consecrate to truth and liberty, –
Deserting these, thou leavest me to grieve,
Thus having been, that thou shouldst cease to be.

FEELINGS OF A REPUBLICAN ON THE FALL OF BONAPARTE

I HATED thee, fallen tyrant! I did groan
To think that a most unambitious slave,
Like thou, shouldst dance and revel on the grave
Of Liberty. Thou mightst have built thy throne
Where it had stood even now: thou didst prefer
A frail and bloody pomp which Time has swept
In fragments towards Oblivion. Massacre,
For this I prayed, would on thy sleep have crept,
Treason and Slavery, Rapine, Fear, and Lust,
And stifled thee, their minister. I know
Too late, since thou and France are in the dust,
That Virtue owns a more eternal foe
Than Force or Fraud: old Custom, legal Crime,
And bloody Faith the foulest birth of Time.

LINES

I

THE cold earth slept below,
  Above the cold sky shone;
And all around, with a chilling sound,
  From caves of ice and fields of snow,
  The breath of night like death did flow
    Beneath the sinking moon.

II

The wintry hedge was black,
  The green grass was not seen,
The birds did rest on the bare thorn's breast,
  Whose roots, beside the pathway track,
  Had bound their folds o'er many a crack
    Which the frost had made between.

III

Thine eyes glowed in the glare
  Of the moon's dying light;
As a fen-fire's beam on a sluggish stream
  Gleams dimly, so the moon shone there,
  And it yellowed the strings of thy raven hair,
    That shook in the wind of night.

IV

The moon made thy lips pale, beloved –
  The wind made thy bosom chill –
The night did shed on thy dear head
  Its frozen dew, and thou didst lie
  Where the bitter breath of the naked sky
    Might visit thee at will.

ALASTOR; OR THE SPIRIT OF
SOLITUDE

*Nondum amabam, et amare amabam, quaerebam quid
amarem, amans amare. – Confess. St August*

EARTH, ocean, air, belovèd brotherhood!
If our great Mother has imbued my soul
With aught of natural piety to feel
Your love, and recompense the boon with mine;
If dewy morn, and odorous noon, and even,
With sunset and its gorgeous ministers,
And solemn midnight's tingling silentness;
If autumn's hollow sighs in the sere wood,
And winter robing with pure snow and crowns
Of starry ice the grey grass and bare boughs;
If spring's voluptuous pantings when she breathes
Her first sweet kisses, have been dear to me;
If no bright bird, insect, or gentle beast
I consciously have injured, but still loved
And cherished these my kindred; then forgive
This boast, belovèd brethren, and withdraw
No portion of your wonted favour now!

Mother of this unfathomable world!
Favour my solemn song, for I have loved
Thee ever, and thee only; I have watched
Thy shadow, and the darkness of thy steps,
And my heart ever gazes on the depth
Of thy deep mysteries. I have made my bed
In charnels and on coffins, where black death
Keeps record of the trophies won from thee,
Hoping to still these obstinate questionings

Of thee and thine, by forcing some lone ghost
Thy messenger, to render up the tale
Of what we are. In lone and silent hours,
When night makes a weird sound of its own stillness,
Like an inspired and desperate alchymist
Staking his very life on some dark hope,
Have I mixed awful talk and asking looks
With my most innocent love, until strange tears
Uniting with those breathless kisses, made
Such magic as compels the charmèd night
To render up thy charge: . . . and, though ne'er yet
Thou hast unveiled thy inmost sanctuary,
Enough from incommunicable dream,
And twilight phantasms, and deep noon-day thought,
Has shone within me, that serenely now
And moveless, as a long-forgotten lyre
Suspended in the solitary dome
Of some mysterious and deserted fane,
I wait thy breath, Great Parent, that my strain
May modulate with murmurs of the air,
And motions of the forests and the sea,
And voice of living beings, and woven hymns
Of night and day, and the deep heart of man.

There was a Poet whose untimely tomb
No human hands with pious reverence reared,
But the charmed eddies of autumnal winds
Built o'er his mouldering bones a pyramid
Of mouldering leaves in the waste wilderness: –
A lovely youth, – no mourning maiden decked
With weeping flowers, or votive cypress wreath,
The lone couch of his everlasting sleep: –
Gentle, and brave, and generous, – no lorn bard
Breathed o'er his dark fate one melodious sigh:

He lived, he died, he sung, in solitude.
Strangers have wept to hear his passionate notes,
And virgins, as unknown he passed, have pined
And wasted for fond love of his wild eyes.
The fire of those soft orbs has ceased to burn,
And Silence, too enamoured of that voice,
Locks its mute music in her rugged cell.

By solemn vision, and bright silver dream,
His infancy was nurtured. Every sight
And sound from the vast earth and ambient air,
Sent to his heart its choicest impulses.
The fountains of divine philosophy
Fled not his thirsting lips, and all of great,
Or good, or lovely, which the sacred past
In truth or fable consecrates, he felt
And knew. When early youth had passed, he left
His cold fireside and alienated home
To seek strange truths in undiscovered lands.
Many a wide waste and tangled wilderness
Has lured his fearless steps; and he has bought
With his sweet voice and eyes, from savage men,
His rest and food. Nature's most secret steps
He like her shadow has pursued, where'er
The red volcano overcanopies
Its fields of snow and pinnacles of ice
With burning smoke, or where bitumen lakes
On black bare pointed islets ever beat
With sluggish surge, or where the secret caves
Rugged and dark, winding among the springs
Of fire and poison, inaccessible
To avarice or pride, their starry domes
Of diamond and of gold expand above
Numberless and immeasurable halls,

Frequent with crystal column, and clear shrines
Of pearl, and thrones radiant with chrysolite.
Nor had that scene of ampler majesty
Than gems or gold, the varying roof of heaven
And the green earth lost in his heart its claims
To love and wonder; he would linger long
In lonesome vales, making the wild his home,
Until the doves and squirrels would partake
From his innocuous hand his bloodless food,
Lured by the gentle meaning of his looks,
And the wild antelope, that starts whene'er
The dry leaf rustles in the brake, suspend
Her timid steps to gaze upon a form
More graceful than her own.
                His wandering step
Obedient to high thoughts, has visited
The awful ruins of the days of old:
Athens, and Tyre, and Balbec, and the waste
Where stood Jerusalem, the fallen towers
Of Babylon, the eternal pyramids,
Memphis and Thebes, and whatsoe'er of strange
Sculptured on alabaster obelisk,
Or jasper tomb, or mutilated sphynx,
Dark Aethiopia in her desert hills
Conceals. Among the ruined temples there,
Stupendous columns, and wild images
Of more than man, where marble daemons watch
The Zodiac's brazen mystery, and dead men
Hang their mute thoughts on the mute walls around,
He lingered, poring on memorials
Of the world's youth, through the long burning day
Gazed on those speechless shapes, nor, when the moon
Filled the mysterious halls with floating shades
Suspended he that task, but ever gazed

And gazed, till meaning on his vacant mind
Flashed like strong inspiration, and he saw
The thrilling secrets of the birth of time.

Meanwhile an Arab maiden brought his food,
Her daily portion, from her father's tent,
And spread her matting for his couch, and stole
From duties and repose to tend his steps: –
Enamoured, yet not daring for deep awe
To speak her love: – and watched his nightly sleep,
Sleepless herself, to gaze upon his lips
Parted in slumber, whence the regular breath
Of innocent dreams arose: then, when red morn
Made paler the pale moon, to her cold home
Wildered, and wan, and panting, she returned.

The Poet wandering on, through Arabie
And Persia, and the wild Carmanian waste,
And o'er the aërial mountains which pour down
Indus and Oxus from their icy caves,
In joy and exultation held his way;
Till in the vale of Cashmire, far within
Its loneliest dell, where odorous plants entwine
Beneath the hollow rocks a natural bower,
Beside a sparkling rivulet he stretched
His languid limbs. A vision on his sleep
There came, a dream of hopes that never yet
Had flushed his cheek. He dreamed a veilèd maid
Sate near him, talking in low solemn tones.
Her voice was like the voice of his own soul
Heard in the calm of thought; its music long,
Like woven sounds of streams and breezes, held
His inmost sense suspended in its web
Of many-coloured woof and shifting hues.

Knowledge and truth and virtue were her theme,
And lofty hopes of divine liberty,
Thoughts the most dear to him, and poesy,
Herself a poet. Soon the solemn mood
Of her pure mind kindled through all her frame
A permeating fire: wild numbers then
She raised, with voice stifled in tremulous sobs
Subdued by its own pathos: her fair hands
Were bare alone, sweeping from some strange harp
Strange symphony, and in their branching veins
The eloquent blood told an ineffable tale.
The beating of her heart was heard to fill
The pauses of her music, and her breath
Tumultuously accorded with those fits
Of intermitted song. Sudden she rose,
As if her heart impatiently endured
Its bursting burthen: at the sound he turned,
And saw by the warm light of their own life
Her glowing limbs beneath the sinuous veil
Of woven wind, her outspread arms now bare,
Her dark locks floating in the breath of night,
Her beamy bending eyes, her parted lips
Outstretched, and pale, and quivering eagerly.
His strong heart sunk and sickened with excess
Of love. He reared his shuddering limbs and quelled
His gasping breath, and spread his arms to meet
Her panting bosom: . . . she drew back a while,
Then, yielding to the irresistible joy,
With frantic gesture and short breathless cry
Folded his frame in her dissolving arms.
Now blackness veiled his dizzy eyes, and night
Involved and swallowed up the vision; sleep,
Like a dark flood suspended in its course,
Rolled back its impulse on his vacant brain.

Roused by the shock he started from his trance –
The cold white light of morning, the blue moon
Low in the west, the clear and garish hills,
The distinct valley and the vacant woods,
Spread round him where he stood. Whither have fled
The hues of heaven that canopied his bower
Of yesternight? The sounds that soothed his sleep,
The mystery and the majesty of Earth,
The joy, the exultation? His wan eyes
Gaze on the empty scene as vacantly
As ocean's moon looks on the moon in heaven.
The spirit of sweet human love has sent
A vision to the sleep of him who spurned
Her choicest gifts. He eagerly pursues
Beyond the realms of dream that fleeting shade;
He overleaps the bounds. Alas! Alas!
Were limbs, and breath, and being intertwined
Thus treacherously? Lost, lost, for ever lost,
In the wide pathless desert of dim sleep,
That beautiful shape! Does the dark gate of death
Conduct to thy mysterious paradise,
O Sleep? Does the bright arch of rainbow clouds,
And pendent mountains seen in the calm lake,
Lead only to a black and watery depth,
While death's blue vault, with loathliest vapours hung,
Where every shade which the foul grave exhales
Hides its dead eye from the detested day,
Conducts, O Sleep, to thy delightful realms?
This doubt with sudden tide flowed on his heart,
The insatiate hope which it awakened, stung
His brain even like despair.
                              While daylight held
The sky, the Poet kept mute conference
With his still soul. At night the passion came,

Like the fierce fiend of a distempered dream,
And shook him from his rest, and led him forth
Into the darkness. – As an eagle grasped
In folds of the green serpent, feels her breast
Burn with the poison, and precipitates
Through night and day, tempest, and calm, and cloud,
Frantic with dizzying anguish, her blind flight
O'er the wide aëry wilderness: thus driven
By the bright shadow of that lovely dream,
Beneath the cold glare of the desolate night,
Through tangled swamps and deep precipitous dells,
Startling with careless step the moonlight snake,
He fled. Red morning dawned upon his flight,
Shedding the mockery of its vital hues
Upon his cheek of death. He wandered on
Till vast Aornos seen from Petra's steep
Hung o'er the low horizon like a cloud;
Through Balk, and where the desolated tombs
Of Parthian kings scatter to every wind
Their wasting dust, wildly he wandered on,
Day after day a weary waste of hours,
Bearing within his life the brooding care
That ever fed on its decaying flame.
And now his limbs were lean; his scattered hair
Sered by the autumn of strange suffering
Sung dirges in the wind; his listless hand
Hung like dead bone within its withered skin;
Life, and the lustre that consumed it, shone
As in a furnace burning secretly
From his dark eyes alone. The cottagers,
Who ministered with human charity
His human wants, beheld with wondering awe
Their fleeting visitant. The mountaineer,
Encountering on some dizzy precipice

That spectral form, deemed that the Spirit of wind
With lightning eyes, and eager breath, and feet
Disturbing not the drifted snow, had paused
In its career: the infant would conceal
His troubled visage in his mother's robe
In terror at the glare of those wild eyes,
To remember their strange light in many a dream
Of after-times; but youthful maidens, taught
By nature, would interpret half the woe
That wasted him, would call him with false names
Brother, and friend, would press his pallid hand
At parting, and watch, dim through tears, the path
Of his departure from their father's door.

At length upon the lone Chorasmian shore
He paused, a wide and melancholy waste
Of putrid marshes. A strong impulse urged
His steps to the sea-shore. A swan was there,
Beside a sluggish stream among the reeds.
It rose as he approached, and with strong wings
Scaling the upward sky, bent its bright course
High over the immeasurable main.
His eyes pursued its flight. – 'Thou hast a home,
Beautiful bird; thou voyagest to thine home,
Where thy sweet mate will twine her downy neck
With thine, and welcome thy return with eyes
Bright in the lustre of their own fond joy.
And what am I that I should linger here,
With voice far sweeter than thy dying notes,
Spirit more vast than thine, frame more attuned
To beauty, wasting these surpassing powers
In the deaf air, to the blind earth, and heaven
That echoes not my thoughts?' A gloomy smile
Of desperate hope wrinkled his quivering lips.

For sleep, he knew, kept most relentlessly
Its precious charge, and silent death exposed,
Faithless perhaps as sleep, a shadowy lure,
With doubtful smile mocking its own strange charms.

Startled by his own thoughts he looked around.
There was no fair fiend near him, not a sight
Or sound of awe but in his own deep mind.
A little shallop floating near the shore
Caught the impatient wandering of his gaze.
It had been long abandoned, for its sides
Gaped wide with many a rift, and its frail joints
Swayed with the undulations of the tide.
A restless impulse urged him to embark
And meet lone Death on the drear ocean's waste;
For well he knew that mighty Shadow loves
The slimy caverns of the populous deep.

The day was fair and sunny, sea and sky
Drank its inspiring radiance, and the wind
Swept strongly from the shore, blackening the waves.
Following his eager soul, the wanderer
Leaped in the boat, he spread his cloak aloft
On the bare mast, and took his lonely seat,
And felt the boat speed o'er the tranquil sea
Like a torn cloud before the hurricane.

As one that in a silver vision floats
Obedient to the sweep of odorous winds
Upon the resplendent clouds, so rapidly
Among the dark and ruffled waters fled
The straining boat. – A whirlwind swept it on,
With fierce gusts and precipitating force,
Through the white ridges of the chafèd sea.

The waves arose. Higher and higher still
Their fierce necks writhed beneath the tempest's sourge
Like serpents struggling in a vulture's grasp.
Calm and rejoicing in the fearful war
Of wave ruining on wave, and blast on blast
Descending, and black flood on whirlpool driven
With dark obliterating course, he sate:
As if their genii were the ministers
Appointed to conduct him to the light
Of those belovèd eyes, the Poet sate
Holding the steady helm. Evening came on,
The beams of sunset hung their rainbow hues
High 'mid the shifting domes of sheeted spray
That canopied his path o'er the waste deep;
Twilight, ascending slowly from the east,
Entwined in duskier wreaths her braided locks
O'er the fair front and radiant eyes of day;
Night followed, clad with stars. On every side
More horribly the multitudinous streams
Of ocean's mountainous waste to mutual way
Rushed in dark tumult thundering, as to mock
The calm and spangled sky. The little boat
Still fled before the storm; still fled, like foam
Down the steep cataract of a wintry river;
Now pausing on the edge of the riven wave;
Now leaving far behind the bursting mass
That fell, convulsing ocean: safely fled –
As if that frail and wasted human form,
Had been an elemental god.
                              At midnight
The moon arose: and lo! the ethereal cliffs
Of Caucasus, whose icy summits shone
Among the stars like sunlight, and around
Whose caverned base the whirlpools and the waves

Bursting and eddying irresistibly
Rage and resound for ever. – Who shall save? –
The boat fled on, – the boiling torrent drove, –
The crags closed round with black and jaggèd arms,
The shattered mountain overhung the sea,
And faster still, beyond all human speed,
Suspended on the sweep of the smooth wave,
The little boat was driven. A cavern there
Yawned, and amid its slant and winding depths
Ingulfed the rushing sea. The boat fled on
With unrelaxing speed. – 'Vision and Love!'
The Poet cried aloud, 'I have beheld
The path of thy departure. Sleep and death
Shall not divide us long!'

                    The boat pursued
The windings of the cavern. Daylight shone
At length upon that gloomy river's flow;
Now, where the fiercest war among the waves
Is calm, on the unfathomable stream
The boat moved slowly. Where the mountain, riven,
Exposed those black depths to the azure sky,
Ere yet the flood's enormous volume fell
Even to the base of Caucasus, with sound
That shook the everlasting rocks, the mass
Filled with one whirlpool all that ample chasm;
Stair above stair the eddying waters rose,
Circling immeasurably fast, and laved
With alternating dash the gnarlèd roots
Of mighty trees, that stretched their giant arms
In darkness over it. I' the midst was left,
Reflecting, yet distorting every cloud,
A pool of treacherous and tremendous calm.
Seized by the sway of the ascending stream,

With dizzy swiftness, round, and round, and round,
Ridge after ridge the straining boat arose,
Till on the verge of the extremest curve,
Where, through an opening of the rocky bank,
The waters overflow, and a smooth spot
Of glassy quiet mid those battling tides
Is left, the boat paused shuddering. – Shall it sink
Down the abyss? Shall the reverting stress
Of that resistless gulf embosom it?
Now shall it fall? – A wandering stream of wind,
Breathed from the west, has caught the expanded sail,
And, lo! with gentle motion, between banks
Of mossy slope, and on a placid stream,
Beneath a woven grove it sails, and, hark!
The ghastly torrent mingles its far roar,
With the breeze murmuring in the musical woods.
Where the embowering trees recede, and leave
A little space of green expanse, the cove
Is closed by meeting banks, whose yellow flowers
For ever gaze on their own drooping eyes,
Reflected in the crystal calm. The wave
Of the boat's motion marred their pensive task,
Which nought but vagrant bird, or wanton wind,
Or falling spear-grass, or their own decay
Had e'er disturbed before. The Poet longed
To deck with their bright hues his withered hair,
But on his heart its solitude returned,
And he forbore. Not the strong impulse hid
In those flushed cheeks, bent eyes, and shadowy frame
Had yet performed its ministry: it hung
Upon his life, as lightning in a cloud
Gleams, hovering ere it vanish, ere the floods
Of night close over it.

                              The noonday sun
Now shone upon the forest, one vast mass
Of mingling shade, whose brown magnificence
A narrow vale embosoms. There, huge caves,
Scooped in the dark base of their aëry rocks
Mocking its moans, respond and roar for ever.
The meeting boughs and implicated leaves
Wove twilight o'er the Poet's path, as led
By love, or dream, or god, or mightier Death,
He sought in Nature's dearest haunt, some bank,
Her cradle, and his sepulchre. More dark
And dark the shades accumulate. The oak,
Expanding its immense and knotty arms,
Embraces the light beech. The pyramids
Of the tall cedar overarching, frame
Most solemn domes within, and far below.
Like clouds suspended in an emerald sky,
The ash and the acacia floating hang
Tremulous and pale. Like restless serpents, clothed
In rainbow and in fire, the parasites,
Starred with ten thousand blossoms, flow around
The grey trunks, and, as gamesome infants' eyes,
With gentle meanings, and most innocent wiles,
Fold their beams round the hearts of those that love,
These twine their tendrils with the wedded boughs
Uniting their close union; the woven leaves
Make net-work of the dark blue light of day,
And the night's noontide clearness, mutable
As shapes in the weird clouds. Soft mossy lawns
Beneath these canopies extend their swells,
Fragrant with perfumed herbs, and eyed with blooms
Minute yet beautiful. One darkest glen
Sends from its woods of musk-rose, twined with jasmine
A soul-dissolving odour, to invite

To some more lovely mystery. Through the dell,
Silence and Twilight here, twin-sisters, keep
Their noonday watch, and sail among the shades,
Like vaporous shapes half seen; beyond, a well,
Dark, gleaming, and of most translucent wave
Images all the woven boughs above,
And each depending leaf, and every speck
Of azure sky, darting between their chasms;
Nor aught else in the liquid mirror laves
Its portraiture, but some inconstant star
Between one foliaged lattice twinkling fair,
Or, painted bird, sleeping beneath the moon,
Or gorgeous insect floating motionless,
Unconscious of the day, ere yet his wings
Have spread their glories to the gaze of noon.

Hither the Poet came. His eyes beheld
Their own wan light through the reflected lines
Of his thin hair, distinct in the dark depth
Of that still fountain; as the human heart,
Gazing in dreams over the gloomy grave,
Sees its own treacherous likeness there. He heard
The motion of the leaves, the grass that sprung
Startled and glanced and trembled even to feel
An unaccustomed presence, and the sound
Of the sweet brook that from the secret springs
Of that dark fountain rose. A Spirit seemed
To stand beside him – clothed in no bright robes
Of shadowy silver or enshrining light,
Borrowed from aught the visible world affords
Of grace, or majesty, or mystery; –
But, undulating woods, and silent well,
And leaping rivulet, and evening gloom
Now deepening the dark shades, for speech assuming,

Held commune with him, as if he and it
Were all that was, – only . . . when his regard
Was raised by intense pensiveness, . . . two eyes,
Two starry eyes, hung in the gloom of thought,
And seemed with their serene and azure smiles
To beckon him.

              Obedient to the light
That shone within his soul, he went, pursuing
The windings of the dell. – The rivulet
Wanton and wild, through many a green ravine
Beneath the forest flowed. Sometimes it fell
Among the moss with hollow harmony
Dark and profound. Now on the polished stones
It danced; like childhood laughing as it went:
Then, through the plain in tranquil wanderings crept,
Reflecting every herb and drooping bud
That overhung its quietness. – 'O stream!
Whose source is inaccessibly profound,
Whither do thy mysterious waters tend?
Thou imagest my life. Thy darksome stillness,
Thy dazzling waves, thy loud and hollow gulfs,
Thy searchless fountain, and invisible course
Have each their type in me: and the wide sky,
And measureless ocean may declare as sôon
What oozy cavern or what wandering cloud
Contains thy waters, as the universe
Tell where these living thoughts reside, when stretched
Upon thy flowers my bloodless limbs shall waste
I' the passing wind!'

              Beside the grassy shore
Of the small stream he went; he did impress
On the green moss his tremulous step, that caught

Strong shuddering from his burning limbs. As one
Roused by some joyous madness from the couch
Of fever, he did not move; yet, not like him,
Forgetful of the grave, where, when the flame
Of his frail exultation shall be spent,
He must descend. With rapid steps he went
Beneath the shade of trees, beside the flow
Of the wild babbling rivulet; and now
The forest's solemn canopies were changed
For the uniform and lightsome evening sky.
Grey rocks did peep from the spare moss, and stemmed
The struggling brook: tall spires of windlestrae
Threw their thin shadows down the rugged slope,
And nought but gnarled roots of ancient pines
Branchless and blasted, clenched with grasping roots
The unwilling soil. A gradual change was here,
Yet ghastly. For, as fast years flow away,
The smooth brow gathers, and the hair grows thin
And white, and where irradiate dewy eyes
Had shone, gleam stony orbs: – so from his steps
Bright flowers departed, and the beautiful shade
Of the green groves, with all their odorous winds
And musical motions. Calm, he still pursued
The stream, that with a larger volume now
Rolled through the labyrinthine dell; and there
Fretted a path through its descending curves
With its wintry speed. On every side now rose
Rocks, which, in unimaginable forms,
Lifted their black and barren pinnacles
In the light of evening, and, its precipice
Obscuring the ravine, disclosed above,
Mid toppling stones, black gulfs and yawning caves,
Whose windings gave ten thousand various tongues
To the loud stream. Lo! where the pass expands

Its stony jaws, the abrupt mountain breaks,
And seems, with its accumulated crags,
To overhang the world: for wide expand
Beneath the wan stars and descending moon
Islanded seas, blue mountains, mighty streams,
Dim tracts and vast, robed in the lustrous gloom
Of leaden-coloured even, and fiery hills
Mingling their flames with twilight, on the verge
Of the remote horizon. The near scene,
In naked and severe simplicity,
Made contrast with the universe. A pine,
Rock-rooted, stretched athwart the vacancy
Its swinging boughs, to each inconstant blast
Yielding one only response, at each pause
In most familiar cadence, with the howl
The thunder and the hiss of homeless streams
Mingling its solemn song, whilst the broad river,
Foaming and hurrying o'er its rugged path,
Fell into that immeasurable void
Scattering its waters to the passing winds.

Yet the grey precipice and solemn pine
And torrent, were not all; – one silent nook
Was there. Even on the edge of that vast mountain,
Upheld by knotty roots and fallen rocks,
It overlooked in its serenity
The dark earth, and the bending vault of stars.
It was a tranquil spot, that seemed to smile
Even in the lap of horror. Ivy clasped
The fissured stones with its entwining arms,
And did embower with leaves for ever green,
And berries dark, the smooth and even space
Of its inviolated floor, and here

The children of the autumnal whirlwind bore,
In wanton sport, those bright leaves, whose decay,
Red, yellow, or ethereally pale,
Rivals the pride of summer. 'Tis the haunt
Of every gentle wind, whose breath can teach
The wilds to love tranquillity. One step,
One human step alone, has ever broken
The stillness of its solitude: – one voice
Alone inspired its echoes; – even that voice
Which hither came, floating among the winds,
And led the loveliest among human forms
To make their wild haunts the depository
Of all the grace and beauty that endued
Its motions, render up its majesty,
Scatter its music on the unfeeling storm,
And to the damp leaves and blue cavern mould,
Nurses of rainbow flowers and branching moss,
Commit the colours of that varying cheek,
That snowy breast, those dark and drooping eyes.

The dim and hornèd moon hung low, and poured
A sea of lustre on the horizon's verge
That overflowed its mountains. Yellow mist
Filled the unbounded atmosphere, and drank
Wan moonlight even to fulness: not a star
Shone, not a sound was heard; the very winds,
Danger's grim playmates, on that precipice
Slept, clasped in his embrace. – O, storm of death!
Whose sightless speed divides this sullen night:
And thou, colossal Skeleton, that, still
Guiding its irresistible career
In thy devastating omnipotence,
Art king of this frail world, from the red field
Of slaughter, from the reeking hospital,

The patriot's sacred couch, the snowy bed
Of innocence, the scaffold and the throne,
A mighty voice invokes thee. Ruin calls
His brother Death. A rare and regal prey
He hath prepared, prowling around the world;
Glutted with which thou mayst repose, and men
Go to their graves like flowers or creeping worms,
Nor ever more offer at thy dark shrine
The unheeded tribute of a broken heart.

When on the threshold of the green recess
The wanderer's footsteps fell, he knew that death
Was on him. Yet a little, ere it fled,
Did he resign his high and mighty soul
To images of the majestic past,
That paused within his passive being now,
Like winds that bear sweet music, when they breathe
Through some dim latticed chamber. He did place
His pale lean hand upon the rugged trunk
Of the old pine. Upon an ivied stone
Reclined his languid head, his limbs did rest,
Diffused and motionless, on the smooth brink
Of that obscurest chasm; – and thus he lay,
Surrendering to their final impulses
The hovering powers of life. Hope and despair,
The torturers, slept; no mortal pain or fear
Marred his repose, the influxes of sense,
And his own being unalloyed by pain,
Yet feebler and more feeble, calmly fed
The stream of thought, till he lay breathing there
At peace, and faintly smiling: – his last sight
Was the great moon, which o'er the western line
Of the wide world her mighty horn suspended,
With whose dun beams inwoven darkness seemed

To mingle. Now upon the jaggèd hills
It rests, and still as the divided frame
Of the vast meteor sunk, the Poet's blood,
That ever beat in mystic sympathy
With nature's ebb and flow, grew feebler still:
And when two lessening points of light alone
Gleamed through the darkness, the alternate gasp
Of his faint respiration scarce did stir
The stagnate night: – till the minutest ray
Was quenched, the pulse yet lingered in his heart.
It paused – it fluttered. But when heaven remained
Utterly black, the murky shades involved
An image, silent, cold, and motionless,
As their own voiceless earth and vacant air.
Even as a vapour fed with golden beams
That ministered on sunlight, ere the west
Eclipses it, was now that wondrous frame –
No sense, no motion, no divinity –
A fragile lute, on whose harmonious strings
The breath of heaven did wander – a bright stream
Once fed with many-voicèd waves – a dream
Of youth, which night and time have quenched for ever,
Still, dark, and dry, and unremembered now.

O, for Medea's wondrous alchemy,
Which wheresoe'er it fell made the earth gleam
With bright flowers, and the wintry boughs exhale
From vernal blooms fresh fragrance! O, that God,
Profuse of poisons, would concede the chalice
Which but one living man has drained, who now,
Vessel of deathless wrath, a slave that feels
No proud exemption in the blighting curse
He bears, over the world wanders for ever,
Lone as incarnate death! O, that the dream
Of dark magician in his visioned cave,

Raking the cinders of a crucible
For life and power, even when his feeble hand
Shakes in its last decay, were the true law
Of this so lovely world! But thou art fled
Like some frail exhalation; which the dawn
Robes in its golden beams, – ah! thou hast fled!
The brave, the gentle, and the beautiful,
The child of grace and genius. Heartless things
Are done and said i' the world, and many worms
And beasts and men live on, and mighty Earth
From sea and mountain, city and wilderness,
In vesper low or joyous orison,
Lifts still its solemn voice: – but thou art fled –
Thou canst no longer know or love the shapes
Of this phantasmal scene, who have to thee
Been purest ministers, who are, alas!
Now thou art not. Upon those pallid lips
So sweet even in their silence, on those eyes
That image sleep in death, upon that form
Yet safe from the worm's outrage, let no tear
Be shed – not even in thought. Nor, when those hues
Are gone, and those divinest lineaments,
Worn by the senseless wind, shall live alone
In the frail pauses of this simple strain,
Let not high verse, mourning the memory
Of that which is no more, or painting's woe
Or sculpture, speak in feeble imagery
Their own cold powers. Art and eloquence,
And all the shows o' the world are frail and vain
To weep a loss that turns their lights to shade.
It is a woe too 'deep for tears', when all
Is reft at once, when some surpassing Spirit,
Whose light adorned the world around it, leaves
Those who remain behind, not sobs or groans,

The passionate tumult of a clinging hope;
But pale despair and cold tranquillity,
Nature's vast frame, the web of human things,
Birth and the grave, that are not as they were.

HYMN TO INTELLECTUAL BEAUTY

I

THE awful shadow of some unseen Power
   Floats though unseen among us, – visiting
   This various world with as inconstant wing
As summer winds that creep from flower to flower, –
Like moonbeams that behind some piny mountain shower,
     It visits with inconstant glance
     Each human heart and countenance;
Like hues and harmonies of evening, –
     Like clouds in starlight widely spread, –
     Like memory of music fled, –
     Like aught that for its grace may be
Dear, and yet dearer for its mystery.

II

Spirit of BEAUTY, that dost consecrate
   With thine own hues all thou dost shine upon
   Of human thought or form, – where art thou gone?
Why dost thou pass away and leave our state,
This dim vast vale of tears, vacant and desolate?
     Ask why the sunlight not for ever
     Weaves rainbows o'er yon mountain-river,
Why aught should fail and fade that once is shown,
     Why fear and dream and death and birth
     Cast on the daylight of this earth
     Such gloom, – why man has such a scope
For love and hate, despondency and hope?

III

No voice from some sublimer world hath ever
   To sage or poet these responses given –

Therefore the names of Demon, Ghost, and Heaven,
Remain the records of their vain endeavour,
Frail spells – whose uttered charm might not avail to sever,
      From all we hear and all we see,
      Doubt, chance, and mutability.
Thy light alone – like mist o'er mountains driven,
      Or music by the night-wind sent
      Through strings of some still instrument,
      Or moonlight on a midnight stream,
Gives grace and truth to life's unquiet dream.

IV

Love, Hope, and Self-esteem, like clouds depart
      And come, for some uncertain moments lent.
      Man were immortal, and omnipotent,
Didst thou, unknown and awful as thou art,
Keep with thy glorious train firm state within his heart.
      Thou messenger of sympathies,
      That wax and wane in lovers' eyes –
Thou – that to human thought art nourishment,
      Like darkness to a dying flame!
      Depart not as thy shadow came,
      Depart not – lest the grave should be,
Like life and fear, a dark reality.

V

While yet a boy I sought for ghosts, and sped
      Through many a listening chamber, cave and ruin,
      And starlight wood, with fearful steps pursuing
Hopes of high talk with the departed dead.
I called on poisonous names with which our youth is fed;
      I was not heard – I saw them not –
      When musing deeply on the lot
Of life, at that sweet time when winds are wooing

All vital things that wake to bring
News of birds and blossoming, –
Sudden, thy shadow fell on me;
I shrieked, and clasped my hands in ecstasy!

VI

I vowed that I would dedicate my powers
.To thee and thine – have I not kept the vow?
With beating heart and streaming eyes, even now
I call the phantoms of a thousand hours
Each from his voiceless grave: they have in visioned bowers
Of studious zeal or love's delight
Outwatched with me the envious night –
They know that never joy illumed my brow
Unlinked with hope that thou wouldst free
This world from its dark slavery,
That Thou – O awful LOVELINESS,
Wouldst give whate'er these words cannot express.

VII

The day becomes more solemn and serene
When noon is past – there is a harmony
In autumn, and a lustre in its sky,
Which through the summer is not heard or seen,
As if it could not be, as if it had not been!
Thus let thy power, which like the truth
Of nature on my passive youth
Descended, to my onward life supply
Its calm – to one who worships thee,
And every form containing thee,
Whom, SPIRIT fair, thy spells did bind
To fear himself, and love all human kind.

MONT BLANC

I

THE everlasting universe of things
Flows through the mind, and rolls its rapid waves,
Now dark – now glittering – now reflecting gloom –
Now lending splendour, where from secret springs
The source of human thought its tribute brings
Of waters, – with a sound but half its own,
Such as a feeble brook will oft assume
In the wild woods, among the mountains lone,
Where waterfalls around it leap for ever,
Where woods and winds contend, and a vast river
Over its rocks ceaselessly bursts and raves.

II

Thus thou, Ravine of Arve – dark, deep Ravine –
Thou many-coloured, many-voicèd vale,
Over whose pines, and crags, and caverns sail
Fast cloud-shadows and sunbeams: awful scene,
Where Power in likeness of the Arve comes down
From the ice-gulfs that gird his secret throne,
Bursting through these dark mountains like the flame
Of lightning through the tempest; – thou dost lie,
Thy giant brood of pines around thee clinging,
Children of elder time, in whose devotion
The chainless winds still come and ever came
To drink their odours, and their mighty swinging
To hear – an old and solemn harmony;
Thine earthly rainbows stretched across the sweep
Of the aethereal waterfall, whose veil
Robes some unsculptured image; the strange sleep
Which when the voices of the desert fail

Wraps all in its own deep eternity; –
Thy caverns echoing to the Arve's commotion,
A loud, lone sound no other sound can tame;
Thou art pervaded with that ceaseless motion,
Thou art the path of that unresting sound –
Dizzy Ravine! and when I gaze on thee
I seem as in a trance sublime and strange
To muse on my own separate fantasy,
My own, my human mind, which passively
Now renders and receives fast influencings,
Holding an unremitting interchange
With the clear universe of things around;
One legion of wild thoughts, whose wandering wings
Now float above thy darkness, and now rest
Where that or thou art no unbidden guest,
In the still cave of the witch Poesy,
Seeking among the shadows that pass by
Ghosts of all things that are, some shade of thee,
Some phantom, some faint image; till the breast
From which they fled recalls them, thou art there!

III

Some say that gleams of a remoter world
Visit the soul in sleep, – that death is slumber,
And that its shapes the busy thoughts outnumber
Of those who wake and live. – I look on high;
Has some unknown omnipotence unfurled
The veil of life and death? or do I lie
In dream, and does the mightier world of sleep
Spread far around and inaccessibly
Its circles? For the very spirit fails,
Driven like a homeless cloud from steep to steep
That vanishes among the viewless gales!
Far, far above, piercing the infinite sky,

Mont Blanc appears, – still, snowy, and serene –
Its subject mountains their unearthly forms
Pile around it, ice and rock; broad vales between
Of frozen floods, unfathomable deeps,
Blue as the overhanging heaven, that spread
And wind among the accumulated steeps;
A desert peopled by the storms alone,
Save when the eagle brings some hunter's bone,
And the wolf tracks her there – how hideously
Its shapes are heaped around! rude, bare, and high,
Ghastly, and scarred, and riven. – Is this the scene
Where the old Earthquake-daemon taught her young
Ruin? Were these their toys? or did a sea
Of fire envelop once this silent snow?
None can reply – all seems eternal now.
The wilderness has a mysterious tongue
Which teaches awful doubt, or faith so mild,
So solemn, so serene, that man may be,
But for such faith, with nature reconciled;
Thou hast a voice, great Mountain, to repeal
Large codes of fraud and woe; not understood
By all, but which the wise, and great, and good
Interpret, or make felt, or deeply feel.

IV

The fields, the lakes, the forests, and the streams,
Ocean, and all the living things that dwell
Within the daedal earth; lightning, and rain,
Earthquake, and fiery flood, and hurricane,
The torpor of the year when feeble dreams
Visit the hidden buds, or dreamless sleep
Holds every future leaf and flower; – the bound
With which from that detested trance they leap;
The works and ways of man, their death and birth,

And that of him and all that his may be;
All things that move and breathe with toil and sound
Are born and die; revolve, subside, and swell.
Power dwells apart in its tranquillity,
Remote, serene, and inaccessible:
And *this*, the naked countenance of earth,
On which I gaze, even these primaeval mountains
Teach the adverting mind. The glaciers creep
Like snakes that watch their prey, from their far fountains,
Slow rolling on; there, many a precipice,
Frost and the Sun in scorn of mortal power
Have piled: dome, pyramid, and pinnacle,
A city of death, distinct with many a tower
And wall impregnable of beaming ice.
Yet not a city, but a flood of ruin
Is there, that from the boundaries of the sky
Rolls its perpetual stream; vast pines are strewing
Its destined path, or in the mangled soil
Branchless and shattered stand; the rocks, drawn down
From yon remotest waste, have overthrown
The limits of the dead and living world,
Never to be reclaimed. The dwelling-place
Of insects, beasts, and birds, becomes its spoil
Their food and their retreat for ever gone,
So much of life and joy is lost. The race
Of man flies far in dread; his work and dwelling
Vanish, like smoke before the tempest's stream,
And their place is not known. Below, vast caves
Shine in the rushing torrents' restless gleam,
Which from those secret chasms in tumult welling
Meet in the vale, and one majestic River,
The breath and blood of distant lands, for ever
Rolls its loud waters to the ocean-waves,
Breathes its swift vapours to the circling air.

V

Mont Blanc yet gleams on high: – the power is there,
The still and solemn power of many sights,
And many sounds, and much of life and death,
In the calm darkness of the moonless nights,
In the lone glare of day, the snows descend
Upon that Mountain; none beholds them there,
Nor when the flakes burn in the sinking sun,
Or the star-beams dart through them: – Winds contend
Silently there, and heap the snow with breath
Rapid and strong, but silently! Its home
The voiceless lightning in these solitudes
Keeps innocently, and like vapour broods
Over the snow. The secret Strength of things
Which governs thought, and to the infinite dome
Of Heaven is as a law, inhabits thee!
And what were thou, and earth, and stars, and sea,
If to the human mind's imaginings
Silence and solitude were vacancy?

TO CONSTANTIA, SINGING

I

THUS to be lost and thus to sink and die,
  Perchance were death indeed! – Constantia, turn!
In thy dark eyes a power like light doth lie,
  Even though the sounds which were thy voice, which
    burn
Between thy lips, are laid to sleep;
  Within thy breath, and on thy hair, like odour, it is yet,
And from thy touch like fire doth leap.
  Even while I write, my burning cheeks are wet,
  Alas, that the torn heart can bleed, but not forget!

II

A breathless awe, like the swift change
  Unseen, but felt in youthful slumbers,
Wild, sweet, but uncommunicably strange,
  Thou breathest now in fast ascending numbers.
The cope of heaven seems rent and cloven
  By the enchantment of thy strain,
And on my shoulders wings are woven,
  To follow its sublime career
Beyond the mighty moons that wane
  Upon the verge of Nature's utmost sphere,
  Till the world's shadowy walls are past and disappear.

III

Her voice is hovering o'er my soul – it lingers
  O'ershadowing it with soft and lulling wings,
The blood and life within those snowy fingers
  Teach witchcraft to the instrumental strings.
My brain is wild, my breath comes quick –

The blood is listening in my frame,
And thronging shadows, fast and thick,
    Fall on my overflowing eyes;
My heart is quivering like a flame;
    As morning dew, that in the sunbeam dies,
    I am dissolved in these consuming ecstasies.

IV

I have no life, Constantia, now, but thee,
    Whilst, like the world-surrounding air, thy song
Flows on, and fills all things with melody. –
    Now is thy voice a tempest swift and strong,
On which, like one in trance upborne,
    Secure o'er rocks and waves I sweep,
Rejoicing like a cloud of morn.
    Now 'tis the breath of summer night,
Which when the starry waters sleep,
    Round western isles, with incense-blossoms bright,
    Lingering, suspends my soul in its voluptuous flight.

From THE REVOLT OF ISLAM

CANTO I

I

WHEN the last hope of trampled France had failed
  Like a brief dream of unremaining glory,
From visions of despair I rose, and scaled
  The peak of an aëreal promontory,
    Whose caverned base with the vexed surge was
      hoary;
And saw the golden dawn break forth, and waken
  Each cloud, and every wave: – but transitory
The calm: for sudden, the firm earth was shaken,
As if by the last wreck its frame were overtaken.

II

So as I stood, one blast of muttering thunder
  Burst in far peals along the waveless deep,
When, gathering fast, around, above, and under,
  Long trains of tremulous mist began to creep,
    Until their complicating lines did steep
The orient sun in shadow: – not a sound
    Was heard; one horrible repose did keep
The forests and the floods, and all around
Darkness more dread than night was poured upon the
  ground.

III

Hark! 'tis the rushing of a wind that sweeps
  Earth and the ocean. See! the lightnings yawn
Deluging Heaven with fire, and the lashed deeps
  Glitter and boil beneath: it rages on,

One mighty stream, whirlwind and waves upthrown,
Lightning, and hail, and darkness eddying by.
There is a pause – the sea-birds, that were gone
Into their caves to shriek, come forth, to spy
What calm has fall'n on earth, what light is in the sky.

IV

For, where the irresistible storm had cloven
    That fearful darkness, the blue sky was seen
Fretted with many a fair cloud interwoven
    Most delicately, and the ocean green,
    Beneath that opening spot of blue serene,
Quivered like burning emerald: calm was spread
    On all below; but far on high, between
Earth and the upper air, the vast clouds fled,
Countless and swift as leaves on autumn's tempest shed.

V

For ever, as the war became more fierce
    Between the whirlwinds and the rack on high,
That spot grew more serene; but light did pierce
    The woof of those white clouds, which seem to lie
    Far, deep, and motionless; while through the sky
The pallid semicircle of the moon
    Passed on, in slow and moving majesty;
Its upper horn arrayed in mists, which soon
But slowly fled, like dew beneath the beams of noon.

VI

I could not choose but gaze; a fascination
    Dwelt in that moon, and sky, and clouds, which drew
My fancy thither, and in expectation
    Of what I knew not, I remained: – the hue
    Of the white moon, amid that heaven so blue,

Suddenly stained with shadow did appear;
   A speck, a cloud, a shape, approaching grew,
Like a great ship in the sun's sinking sphere
Beheld afar at sea, and swift it came anear.

VII

Even like a bark, which from a chasm of mountains,
   Dark, vast, and overhanging, on a river
Which there collects the strength of all its fountains,
   Comes forth, whilst with the speed its frame doth
      quiver,
   Sails, oars, and stream, tending to one endeavour;
So, from that chasm of light a wingèd Form
   On all the winds of heaven approaching ever
Floated, dilating as it came: the storm
Pursued it with fierce blasts, and lightnings swift and
    warm.

VIII

A course precipitous, of dizzy speed,
   Suspending thought and breath; a monstrous sight!
For in the air do I behold indeed
   An Eagle and a Serpent wreathed in fight: –
   And now relaxing its impetuous flight,
Before the aëreal rock on which I stood,
   The Eagle, hovering, wheeled to left and right,
And hung with lingering wings over the flood,
And startled with its yells the wide air's solitude.

IX

A shaft of light upon its wings descended,
   And every golden feather gleamed therein –
Feather and scale, inextricably blended.
   The Serpent's mailed and many-coloured skin

Shone through the plumes its coils were twined within
By many a swoln and knotted fold, and high
   And far, the neck, receding lithe and thin,
Sustained a crested head, which warily
Shifted and glanced before the Eagle's steadfast eye.

X

Around, around, in ceaseless circles wheeling
   With clang of wings and scream, the Eagle sailed
Incessantly – sometimes on high concealing
   Its lessening orbs, sometimes as if it failed,
   Drooped through the air; and still it shrieked and
      wailed,
And casting back its eager head, with beak
   And talon unremittingly assailed
The wreathèd Serpent, who did ever seek
Upon his enemy's heart a mortal wound to wreak.

XI

What life, what power, was kindled and arose
   Within the sphere of that appalling fray!
For, from the encounter of those wondrous foes,
   A vapour like the sea's suspended spray
   Hung gathered in the void air, far away,
Floated the shattered plumes; bright scales did leap,
   Where'er the Eagle's talons made their way,
Like sparks into the darkness; – as they sweep,
Blood stains the snowy foam of the tumultuous deep.

XII

Swift chances in that combat – many a check,
   And many a change, a dark and wild turmoil;
Sometimes the Snake around his enemy's neck
   Locked in stiff rings his adamantine coil,

84

Until the Eagle, faint with pain and toil,
Remitted his strong flight, and near the sea
   Languidly fluttered, hopeless so to foil
His adversary, who then reared on high
His red and burning crest, radiant with victory.

XIII

Then on the white edge of the bursting surge,
   Where they had sunk together, would the Snake
Relax his suffocating grasp, and scourge
   The wind with his wild writhings; for to break
   That chain of torment, the vast bird would shake
The strength of his unconquerable wings
   As in despair, and with his sinewy neck,
Dissolve in sudden shock those linkèd rings,
Then soar – as swift as smoke from a volcano springs.

XIV

Wile baffled wile, and strength encountered strength,
   Thus long, but unprevailing: – the event
Of that portentous fight appeared at length:
   Until the lamp of day was almost spent
   It had endured, when lifeless, stark, and rent,
Hung high that mighty Serpent, and at last
   Fell to the sea, while o'er the continent,
With clang of wings and scream the Eagle passed,
Heavily borne away on the exhausted blast.

XV

And with it fled the tempest, so that ocean
   And earth and sky shone through the atmosphere –
Only, 'twas strange to see the red commotion
   Of waves like mountains o'er the sinking sphere
   Of sunset sweep, and their fierce roar to hear

Amid the calm: down the steep path I wound
   To the sea-shore – the evening was most clear
And beautiful, and there the sea I found
Calm as a cradled child in dreamless slumber bound.

XVI

There was a Woman, beautiful as morning,
   Sitting beneath the rocks, upon the sand
Of the waste sea – fair as one flower adorning
   An icy wilderness – each delicate hand
   Lay crossed upon her bosom, and the band
Of her dark hair had fall'n, and so she sate
   Looking upon the waves; on the bare strand
Upon the sea-mark a small boat did wait,
Fair as herself, like Love by Hope left desolate.

XVII

It seemed that this fair Shape had looked upon
   That unimaginable fight, and now
That her sweet eyes were weary of the sun,
   As brightly it illustrated her woe;
   For in the tears which silently to flow
Paused not, its lustre hung: she watching aye
   The foam-wreaths which the faint tide wove below
Upon the spangled sands, groaned heavily,
And after every groan looked up over the sea.

XVIII

And when she saw the wounded Serpent make
   His path between the waves, her lips grew pale,
Parted, and quivered; the tears ceased to break
   From her immovable eyes; no voice of wail
   Escaped her; but she rose, and on the gale
Loosening her star-bright robe and shadowy hair

Poured forth her voice; the caverns of the vale
That opened to the ocean, caught it there,
And filled with silver sounds the overflowing air.

XIX

She spake in language whose strange melody
    Might not belong to earth. I heard, alone,
What made its music more melodious be,
    The pity and the love of every tone;
    But to the Snake those accents sweet were known
His native tongue and hers; nor did he beat
    The hoar spray idly then, but winding on
Through the green shadows of the waves that meet
Near to the shore, did pause beside her snowy feet.

XX

Then on the sands the Woman sate again,
    And wept and clasped her hands, and all between,
Renewed the unintelligible strain
    Of her melodious voice and eloquent mien;
    And she unveiled her bosom, and the green
And glancing shadows of the sea did play
    O'er its marmoreal depth: – one moment seen,
For ere the next, the Serpent did obey
Her voice, and coiled in rest in her embrace it lay.

XXI

Then she arose, and smiled on me with eyes
    Serene yet sorrowing, like that planet fair,
While yet the daylight lingereth in the skies
    Which cleaves with arrowy beams the dark-red air,
    And said: 'To grieve is wise, but the despair
Was weak and vain which led thee here from sleep:
    This shalt thou know, and more, if thou dost dare

With me and with this Serpent, o'er the deep,
A voyage divine and strange, companionship to keep.'

XXII

Her voice was like the wildest, saddest tone,
 Yet sweet, of some loved voice heard long ago.
I wept. 'Shall this fair woman all alone,
 Over the sea with that fierce Serpent go?
 His head is on her heart, and who can know
How soon he may devour his feeble prey?' –
 Such were my thoughts, when the tide gan to flow;
And that strange boat like the moon's shade did sway
Amid reflected stars that in the waters lay: –

XXIII

A boat of rare device, which had no sail
 But its own curvèd prow of thin moonstone,
Wrought like a web of texture fine and frail,
 To catch those gentlest winds which are not known
 To breathe, but by the steady speed alone
With which it cleaves the sparkling sea; and now
 We are embarked – the mountains hang and frown
Over the starry deep that gleams below,
A vast and dim expanse, as o'er the waves we go.

． ． ．

XLII

'The day passed thus: at night, methought in dream
 A shape of speechless beauty did appear:
It stood like light on a careering stream
 Of golden clouds which shook the atmosphere;
 A wingèd youth, his radiant brow did wear
The Morning Star: a wild dissolving bliss
 Over my frame he breathed, approaching near,

And bent his eyes of kindling tenderness
Near mine, and on my lips impressed a lingering kiss, –

XLIII

'And said: "A Spirit loves thee, mortal maiden,
    How wilt thou prove thy worth?" Then joy and sleep
Together fled, my soul was deeply laden,
    And to the shore I went to muse and weep;
    But as I moved, over my heart did creep
A joy less soft, but more profound and strong
    Than my sweet dream; and it forbade to keep
The path of the sea-shore: that Spirit's tongue
Seemed whispering in my heart, and bore my steps along.

XLIV

'How, to that vast and peopled city led,
    Which was a field of holy warfare then,
I walked among the dying and the dead,
    And shared in fearless deeds with evil men,
    Calm as an angel in the dragon's den –
How I braved death for liberty and truth,
    And spurned at peace, and power, and fame – and
        when
Those hopes had lost the glory of their youth,
How sadly I returned – might move the hearer's ruth:

XLV

'Warm tears throng fast! the tale may not be said –
    Know then, that when this grief had been subdued,
I was not left, like others, cold and dead;
    The Spirit whom I loved, in solitude
    Sustained his child: the tempest-shaken wood,
The waves, the fountains, and the hush of night –
    These were his voice, and well I understood

His smile divine, when the calm sea was bright
With silent stars, and Heaven was breathless with delight.

XLVI

'In lonely glens, amid the roar of rivers,
    When the dim nights were moonless, have I known
Joys which no tongue can tell; my pale lip quivers
    When thought revisits them: – know thou alone,
    That after many wondrous years were flown,
I was awakened by a shriek of woe;
    And over me a mystic robe was thrown,
By viewless hands, and a bright Star did glow
Before my steps – the Snake then met his mortal foe.'

XLVII

'Thou fearest not then the Serpent on thy heart?'
    'Fear it!' she said, with brief and passionate cry,
And spake no more: that silence made me start –
    I looked, and we were sailing pleasantly,
    Swift as a cloud between the sea and sky;
Beneath the rising moon seen far away,
    Mountains of ice, like sapphire, piled on high,
Hemming the horizon round, in silence lay
On the still waters – these we did approach alway.

XLVIII

And swift and swifter grew the vessel's motion,
    So that a dizzy trance fell on my brain –
Wild music woke me: we had passed the ocean
    Which girds the pole, Nature's remotest reign –
    And we glode fast o'er a pellucid plain
Of waters, azure with the noontide day.
    Ethereal mountains shone around – a Fane
Stood in the midst, girt by green isles which lay
On the blue sunny deep, resplendent far away.

CANTO II

I

THE starlight smile of children, the sweet looks
   Of women, the fair breast from which I fed,
The murmur of the unreposing brooks,
   And the green light which, shifting overhead,
   Some tangled bower of vines around me shed,
The shells on the sea-sand, and the wild flowers,
   The lamplight through the rafters cheerly spread,
And on the twining flax – in life's young hours
These sights and sounds did nurse my spirit's folded
    powers.

II

In Argolis, beside the echoing sea,
   Such impulses within my mortal frame
Arose, and they were dear to memory,
   Like tokens of the dead: – but others came
   Soon, in another shape: the wondrous fame
Of the past world, the vital words and deeds
   Of minds whom neither time nor change can tame,
Traditions dark and old, whence evil creeds
Start forth, and whose dim shade a stream of poison feeds.

III

I heard, as all have heard, the various story
   Of human life, and wept unwilling tears.
Feeble historians of its shame and glory,
   False disputants on all its hopes and fears,
   Victims who worshipped ruin, – chroniclers
Of daily scorn, and slaves who loathed their state

Yet, flattering power, had given its ministers
A throne of judgement in the grave: – 'twas fate,
That among such as these my youth should seek its mate.

IV

The land in which I lived, by a fell bane
    Was withered up. Tyrants dwelt side by side,
And stabled in our homes, – until the chain
    Stifled the captive's cry, and to abide
    That blasting curse men had no shame – all vied
In evil, slave and despot; fear with lust
    Strange fellowship through mutual hate had tied,
Like two dark serpents tangled in the dust,
Which on the paths of men their mingling poison thrust.

V

Earth, our bright home, its mountains and its waters,
    And the ethereal shapes which are suspended
Over its green expanse, and those fair daughters,
    The clouds, of Sun and Ocean, who have blended
    The colours of the air since first extended
It cradled the young world, none wandered forth
    To see or feel: a darkness had descended
On every heart: the light which shows its worth,
Must among gentle thoughts and fearless take its birth.

VI

This vital world, this home of happy spirits,
    Was as a dungeon to my blasted kind;
All that despair from murdered hope inherits
    They sought, and in their helpless misery blind,
    A deeper prison and heavier chains did find,
And stronger tyrants: – a dark gulf before,
    The realm of a stern Ruler, yawned; behind,

Terror and Time conflicting drove, and bore
On their tempestuous flood the shrieking wretch from
    shore.

VII

Out of that Ocean's wrecks had Guilt and Woe
    Framed a dark dwelling for their homeless thought,
And, starting at the ghosts which to and fro
    Glide o'er its dim and gloomy strand, had brought
    The worship thence which they each other taught.
Well might men loathe their life, well might they turn
    Even to the ills again from which they sought
Such refuge after death! – well might they learn
To gaze on this fair world with hopeless unconcern!

VIII

For they all pined in bondage; body and soul,
    Tyrant and slave, victim and torturer, bent
Before one Power, to which supreme control
    Over their will by their own weakness lent,
    Made all its many names omnipotent;
All symbols of things evil, all divine;
    And hymns of blood or mockery, which rent
The air from all its fanes, did intertwine
Imposture's impious toils round each discordant shrine.

IX

I heard, as all have heard, life's various story,
    And in no careless heart transcribed the tale;
But, from the sneers of men who had grown hoary
    In shame and scorn, from groans of crowds made pale
    By famine, from a mother's desolate wail
O'er her polluted child, from innocent blood
    Poured on the earth, and brows anxious and pale

With the heart's warfare; did I gather food
To feed my many thoughts: a tameless multitude!

X

I wandered through the wrecks of days departed
    Far by the desolated shore, when even
O'er the still sea and jagged islets darted
    The light of moonrise; in the northern Heaven,
    Among the clouds near the horizon driven,
The mountains lay beneath our planet pale;
    Around me, broken tombs and columns riven
Looked vast in twilight, and the sorrowing gale
Waked in those ruins gray its everlasting wail!

XI

I knew not who had framed these wonders then,
    Nor had I heard the story of their deeds;
But dwellings of a race of mightier men,
    And monuments of less ungentle creeds
    Tell their own tale to him who wisely heeds
The language which they speak; and now, to me
    The moonlight making pale the blooming weeds,
The bright stars shining in the breathless sea,
Interpreted those scrolls of mortal mystery.

XII

Such man has been, and such may yet become!
    Ay, wiser, greater, gentler, even than they
Who on the fragments of yon shattered dome
    Have stamped the sign of power – I felt the sway
    Of the vast stream of ages bear away
My floating thoughts – my heart beat loud and fast –
    Even as a storm let loose beneath the ray
Of the still moon, my spirit onward past
Beneath truth's steady beams upon its tumult cast.

XIII

It shall be thus no more! too long, too long,
　　Sons of the glorious dead, have ye lain bound
In darkness and in ruin! – Hope is strong,
　　Justice and Truth their wingèd child have found –
　　Awake! arise! until the mighty sound
Of your career shall scatter in its gust
　　The thrones of the oppressor, and the ground
Hide the last altar's unregarded dust,
Whose Idol has so long betrayed your impious trust!

· · ·

XXI

An orphan with my parents lived, whose eyes
　　Were lodestars of delight, which drew me home
When I might wander forth; nor did I prize
　　Aught human thing beneath Heaven's mighty dome
　　Beyond this child: so when sad hours were come,
And baffled hope like ice still clung to me,
　　Since kin were cold, and friends had now become
Heartless and false, I turned from all, to be,
Cythna, the only source of tears and smiles to thee.

XXII

What wert thou then? A child most infantine,
　　Yet wandering far beyond that innocent age
In all but its sweet looks and mien divine:
　　Even then, methought, with the world's tyrant rage
　　A patient warfare thy young heart did wage,
When those soft eyes of scarcely conscious thought
　　Some tale, or thine own fancies, would engage
To overflow with tears, or converse fraught

With passion, o'er their depths its fleeting light had
    wrought.

XXIII

She moved upon this earth a shape of brightness,
    A power, that from its objects scarcely drew
One impulse of her being – in her lightness
    Most like some radiant cloud of morning dew,
    Which wanders through the waste air's pathless blue,
To nourish some far desert: she did seem
    Beside me, gathering beauty as she grew,
Like the bright shade of some immortal dream
Which walks, when tempest sleeps, the wave of life's dark
    stream.

XXIV

As mine own shadow was this child to me,
    A second self, far dearer and more fair;
Which clothed in undissolving radiancy
    All those steep paths which languor and despair
    Of human things, had made so dark and bare,
But which I trod alone – nor, till bereft
    Of friends, and overcome by lonely care,
Knew I what solace for that loss was left,
Though by a bitter wound my trusting heart was cleft.

XXV

Once she was dear, now she was all I had
    To love in human life – this playmate sweet,
This child of twelve years old – so she was made
    My sole associate, and her willing feet
    Wandered with mine where earth and ocean meet,
Beyond the aëreal mountains whose vast cells
    The unreposing billows ever beat,

Through forests wide and old, and lawny dells
Where boughs of incense droop over the emerald wells.

XXVI

And warm and light I felt her clasping hand
    When twined in mine: she followed where I went,
Through the lone paths of our immortal land.
    It had no waste but some memorial lent
    Which strung me to my toil – some monument
Vital with mind: then, Cythna by my side,
    Until the bright and beaming day were spent,
Would rest, with looks entreating to abide,
Too earnest and too sweet ever to be denied.

XXVII

And soon I could not have refused her – thus
    For ever, day and night, we two were ne'er
Parted, but when brief sleep divided us:
    And when the pauses of the lulling air
    Of noon beside the sea, had made a lair
For her soothed senses, in my arms she slept,
    And I kept watch over her slumbers there,
While, as the shifting visions o'er her swept,
Amid her innocent rest by turns she smiled and wept.

.   .   .

CANTO XI

I

SHE saw me not – she heard me not – alone
    Upon the mountain's dizzy brink she stood;
She spake not, breathed not, moved not – there was
    thrown

Over her look, the shadow of a mood
   Which only clothes the heart in solitude,
A thought of voiceless depth; – she stood alone,
   Above, the Heavens were spread; – below, the flood
Was murmuring in its caves; – the wind had blown
Her hair apart, through which her eyes and forehead shone.

II

A cloud was hanging o'er the western mountains;
   Before its blue and moveless depth were flying
Gray mists poured forth from the unresting fountains
   Of darkness in the North: – the day was dying: –
   Sudden, the sun shone forth, its beams were lying
Like boiling gold on Ocean, strange to see,
   And on the shattered vapours, which defying
The power of light in vain, tossed restlessly
In the red Heaven, like wrecks in a tempestuous sea.

III

It was a stream of living beams, whose bank
   On either side by the cloud's cleft was made;
And where its chasms that flood of glory drank,
   Its waves gushed forth like fire, and as if swayed
   By some mute tempest, rolled on *her*; the shade
Of her bright image floated on the river
   Of liquid light, which then did end and fade –
Her radiant shape upon its verge did shiver;
Aloft, her flowing hair like strings of flame did quiver.

IV

I stood beside her, but she saw me not –
   She looked upon the sea, and skies, and earth;
Rapture, and love, and admiration wrought

A passion deeper far than tears, or mirth,
  Or speech, or gesture, or whate'er has birth
From common joy; which with the speechless feeling
  That led her there united, and shot forth
From her far eyes a light of deep revealing,
All but her dearest self from my regard concealing.

V

Her lips were parted, and the measured breath
  Was now heard there; – her dark and intricate eyes
Orb within orb, deeper than sleep or death,
  Absorbed the glories of the burning skies,
  Which, mingling with her heart's deep ecstasies,
Burst from her looks and gestures; – and a light
  Of liquid tenderness, like love, did rise
From her whole frame, an atmosphere which quite
Arrayed her in its beams, tremulous and soft and bright.

VI

She would have clasped me to her glowing frame;
  Those warm and odorous lips might soon have shed
On mine the fragrance and the invisible flame
  Which now the cold winds stole; – she would have
    laid
  Upon my languid heart her dearest head;
I might have heard her voice, tender and sweet;
  Her eyes mingling with mine, might soon have fed
My soul with their own joy. – One moment yet
I gazed – we parted then, never again to meet!

VII

Never but once to meet on Earth again!
  She heard me as I fled – her eager tone
Sunk on my heart, and almost wove a chain

Around my will to link it with her own,
　　So that my stern resolve was almost gone.
'I cannot reach thee! whither dost thou fly?
　　My steps are faint – Come back, thou dearest one –
Return, ah me! return!' – The wind passed by
On which those accents died, faint, far, and lingeringly.

．　　．　　．

CANTO XII

XXXII

And with the silence of her eloquent smile,
　　Bade us embark in her divine canoe;
Then at the helm we took our seat, the while
　　Above her head those plumes of dazzling hue
　　Into the winds' invisible stream she threw,
Sitting beside the prow: like gossamer
　　On the swift breath of morn, the vessel flew
O'er the bright whirlpools of that fountain fair,
Whose shores receded fast, whilst we seemed lingering
　　　　there;

XXXIII

Till down that mighty stream, dark, calm, and fleet,
　　Between a chasm of cedarn mountains riven,
Chased by the thronging winds whose viewless feet
　　As swift as twinkling beams, had, under Heaven,
　　From woods and waves wild sounds and odours
　　　　driven,
The boat fled visibly – three nights and days,
　　Borne like a cloud through morn, and noon, and even,

We sailed along the winding watery ways
Of the vast stream, a long and labyrinthine maze.

XXXIV

A scene of joy and wonder to behold
  That river's shapes and shadows changing ever,
When the broad sunrise filled with deepening gold
  Its whirlpools, where all hues did spread and quiver;
  And where melodious falls did burst and shiver
Among rocks clad with flowers, the foam and spray
  Sparkled like stars upon the sunny river,
Or when the moonlight poured a holier day,
One vast and glittering lake around green islands lay.

XXXV

Morn, noon, and even, that boat of pearl outran
  The streams which bore it, like the arrowy cloud
Of tempest, or the speedier thought of man,
  Which flieth forth and cannot make abode;
  Sometimes through forests, deep like night, we glode,
Between the walls of mighty mountains crowned
  With Cyclopean piles, whose turrets proud,
The homes of the departed, dimly frowned
O'er the bright waves which girt their dark foundations
    round.

XXXVI

Sometimes between the wide and flowering meadows,
  Mile after mile we sailed, and 'twas delight
To see far off the sunbeams chase the shadows
  Over the grass; sometimes beneath the night
  Of wide and vaulted caves, whose roofs were bright
With starry gems, we fled, whilst from their deep
  And dark-green chasms, shades beautiful and white,

Amid sweet sounds across our path would sweep,
Like swift and lovely dreams that walk the waves of sleep.

XXXVII

And ever as we sailed, our minds were full
　　Of love and wisdom, which would overflow
In converse wild, and sweet, and wonderful,
　　And in quick smiles whose light would come and go
　　Like music o'er wide waves, and in the flow
Of sudden tears, and in the mute caress –
　　For a deep shade was cleft, and we did know,
That virtue, though obscured on Earth, not less
Survives all mortal change in lasting loveliness.

XXXVIII

Three days and nights we sailed, as thought and feeling
　　Number delightful hours – for through the sky
The spherèd lamps of day and night, revealing
　　New changes and new glories, rolled on high,
　　Sun, Moon, and moonlike lamps, the progeny
Of a diviner Heaven, serene and fair:
　　On the fourth day, wild as a windwrought sea
The stream became, and fast and faster bare
The spirit-wingèd boat, steadily speeding there.

XXXIX

Steady and swift, where the waves rolled like mountains
　　Within the vast ravine, whose rifts did pour
Tumultuous floods from their ten thousand fountains,
　　The thunder of whose earth-uplifting roar
　　Made the air sweep in whirlwinds from the shore,
Calm as a shade, the boat of that fair child
　　Securely fled, that rapid stress before,

Amid the topmost spray, and sunbows wild,
Wreathed in the silver mist: in joy and pride we smiled.

XL

The torrent of that wide and raging river
　　Is passed, and our aëreal speed suspended.
We look behind; a golden mist did quiver
　　Where its wild surges with the lake were blended, –
　　Our bark hung there, as on a line suspended
Between two heavens, – that windless waveless lake
　　Which four great cataracts from four vales, attended
By mists, aye feed; from rocks and clouds they break,
And of that azure sea a silent refuge make.

XLI

Motionless resting on the lake awhile,
　　I saw its marge of snow-bright mountains rear
Their peaks aloft, I saw each radiant isle,
　　And in the midst, afar, even like a sphere
　　Hung in one hollow sky, did there appear
The Temple of the Spirit; on the sound
　　Which issued thence, drawn nearer and more near,
Like the swift moon this glorious earth around,
The charmèd boat approached, and there its haven found.

TO WILLIAM SHELLEY

I

THE billows on the beach are leaping around it,
 The bark is weak and frail,
The sea looks black, and the clouds that bound it
 Darkly strew the gale.
Come with me, thou delightful child,
Come with me, though the wave is wild,
And the winds are loose, we must not stay,
Or the slaves of the law may rend thee away.

II

They have taken thy brother and sister dear,
 They have made them unfit for thee;
They have withered the smile and dried the tear
 Which should have been sacred to me.
To a blighting faith and a cause of crime
They have bound them slaves in youthly prime,
And they will curse my name and thee
Because we fearless are and free.

III

Come thou, belovèd as thou art;
 Another sleepeth still
Near thy sweet mother's anxious heart,
 Which thou with joy shalt fill,
With fairest smiles of wonder thrown
On that which is indeed our own,
And which in distant lands will be
The dearest playmate unto thee.

IV

Fear not the tyrants will rule for ever,
    Or the priests of the evil faith;
They stand on the brink of that raging river,
    Whose waves they have tainted with death.
It is fed from the depth of a thousand dells,
Around them it foams and rages and swells;
And their swords and their sceptres I floating see,
Like wrecks on the surge of eternity.

V

Rest, rest, and shriek not, thou gentle child!
    The rocking of the boat thou fearest,
And the cold spray and the clamour wild? –
    There, sit between us two, thou dearest –
Me and thy mother – well we know
The storm at which thou tremblest so,
With all its dark and hungry graves,
Less cruel than the savage slaves
Who hunt us o'er these sheltering waves.

VI

This hour will in thy memory
    Be a dream of days forgotten long.
We soon shall dwell by the azure sea
Of serene and golden Italy,
Or Greece, the Mother of the free;
    And I will teach thine infant tongue
To call upon those heroes old
In their own language, and will mould
Thy growing spirit in the flame
Of Grecian lore, that by such name
A patriot's birthright thou mayst claim!

ON FANNY GODWIN

HER voice did quiver as we parted,
   Yet knew I not that heart was broken
From which it came, and I departed
   Heeding not the words then spoken.
     Misery – O Misery,
    This world is all too wide for thee.

OZYMANDIAS

I MET a traveller from an antique land
Who said: Two vast and trunkless legs of stone
Stand in the desert . . . Near them, on the sand,
Half sunk, a shattered visage lies, whose frown,
And wrinkled lip, and sneer of cold command,
Tell that its sculptor well those passions read
Which yet survive, stamped on these lifeless things,
The hand that mocked them, and the heart that fed:
And on the pedestal these words appear:
'My name is Ozymandias, king of kings:
Look on my works, ye Mighty, and despair!'
Nothing beside remains. Round the decay
Of that colossal wreck, boundless and bare
The lone and level sands stretch far away.

ON A FADED VIOLET

I

THE odour from the flower is gone;
　　Which like thy kisses breathed on me;
The colour from the flower is flown
　　Which glowed of thee and only thee!

II

A shrivelled, lifeless, vacant form,
　　It lies on my abandoned breast,
And mocks the heart which yet is warm,
　　With cold and silent rest.

III

I weep, – my tears revive it not!
　　I sigh, – it breathes no more on me;
Its mute and uncomplaining lot
　　Is such as mine should be.

From ROSALIND AND HELEN

In silence then they took the way
Beneath the forest's solitude.
It was a vast and antique wood,
Thro' which they took their way;
And the gray shades of evening
O'er that green wilderness did fling
Still deeper solitude.
Pursuing still the path that wound
The vast and knotted trees around
Through which slow shades were wandering,
To a deep lawny dell they came,
To a stone seat beside a spring,
O'er which the columned wood did frame
A roofless temple, like the fane
Where, ere new creeds could faith obtain,
Man's early race once knelt beneath
The overhanging deity.
O'er this fair fountain hung the sky,
Now spangled with rare stars. The snake,
The pale snake, that with eager breath
Creeps here his noontide thirst to slake,
Is beaming with many a mingled hue,
Shed from yon dome's eternal blue,
When he floats on that dark and lucid flood
In the light of his own loveliness;
And the birds that in the fountain dip
Their plumes, with fearless fellowship
Above and round him wheel and hover.
The fitful wind is heard to stir
One solitary leaf on high;
The chirping of the grasshopper

Fills every pause. There is emotion
In all that dwells at noontide here:
Then, through the intricate wild wood,
A maze of life and light and motion
Is woven. But there is stillness now:
Gloom, and the trance of Nature now:
The snake is in his cave asleep;
The birds are on the branches dreaming:
Only the shadows creep:
Only the glow-worm is gleaming:
Only the owls and the nightingales
Wake in this dell when daylight fails,
And gray shades gather in the woods:
And the owls have all fled far away
In a merrier glen to hoot and play,
For the moon is veiled and sleeping now.
The accustomed nightingale still broods
On her accustomed bough,
But she is mute; for her false mate
Has fled and left her desolate.

This silent spot tradition old
Had peopled with the spectral dead.
For the roots of the speaker's hair felt cold
And stiff, as with tremulous lips he told
That a hellish shape at midnight led
The ghost of youth with hoary hair,
And sate on the seat beside him there,
Till a naked child came wandering by,
When the fiend would change to a lady fair!
A fearful tale! The truth was worse:
For here a sister and a brother
Had solemnized a monstrous curse,
Meeting in this fair solitude:

For beneath yon very sky,
Had they resigned to one another
Body and soul. The multitude:
Tracking them to the secret wood,
Tore limb from limb their innocent child,
And stabbed and trampled on its mother;
But the youth, for God's most holy grace,
A priest saved to burn in the market-place.

LINES WRITTEN AMONG THE
EUGANEAN HILLS

MANY a green isle needs must be
In the deep wide sea of Misery,
Or the mariner, worn and wan
Never thus could voyage on –
Day and night, and night and day,
Drifting on his dreary way,
With the solid darkness black
Closing round his vessel's track;
Whilst above the sunless sky,
Big with clouds, hangs heavily,
And behind the tempest fleet
Hurries on with lightning feet,
Riving sail, and cord, and plank,
Till the ship has almost drank
Death from the o'er-brimming deep;
And sinks down, down, like that sleep
When the dreamer seems to be
Weltering through eternity;
And the dim low line before
Of a dark and distant shore
Still recedes, as ever still
Longing with divided will,
But no power to seek or shun,
He is ever drifted on
O'er the unreposing wave
To the haven of the grave.
What, if there no friends will greet;
What, if there no heart will meet
His with love's impatient beat;
Wander whereso'er he may,

Can he dream before that day
To find refuge from distress
In friendship's smile, in love's caress?
Then 'twill wreak him little woe
Whether such there be or no:
Senseless is the breast, and cold,
Which relenting love would fold;
Bloodless are the veins and chill
Which the pulse of pain did fill;
Every little living nerve
That from bitter words did swerve
Round the tortured lips and brow,
Are like sapless leaflets now
Frozen upon December's bough.

On the beach of a northern sea
Which tempests shake eternally,
As once the wretch there lay to sleep,
Lies a solitary heap,
One white skull and seven dry bones,
On the margin of the stones,
Where a few gray rushes stand,
Boundaries of the sea and land:
Nor is heard one voice of wail
But the sea-mews, as they sail
O'er the billows of the gale;
Or the whirlwind up and down
Howling, like a slaughtered town,
When a king in glory rides
Through the pomp of fratricides:
Those unburied bones around
There is many a mournful sound;
There is no lament for him,
Like a sunless vapour, dim,

Who once clothed with life and thought
What now moves nor murmurs not.

Ay, many flowering islands lie
In the water of wide Agony:
To such a one this morn was led,
My bark by soft winds piloted:
'Mid the mountains Euganean
I stood listening to the paean
With which the legioned rooks did hail
The sun's uprise majestical;
Gathering round with wings all hoar,
Through the dewy mist they soar
Like gray shades, till the eastern heaven
Bursts, and then, as clouds of even,
Flecked with fire and azure, lie
In the unfathomable sky,
So their plumes of purple grain,
Starred with drops of golden rain,
Gleam above the sunlight woods,
As in silent multitudes
On the morning's fitful gale
Through the broken mist they sail,
And the vapours cloven and gleaming
Follow, down the dark steep streaming,
Till all is bright, and clear, and still,
Round the solitary hill.

Beneath is spread like a green sea
The waveless plain of Lombardy,
Bounded by the vaporous air,
Islanded by cities fair;
Underneath Day's azure eyes
Ocean's nursling, Venice lies,

A peopled labyrinth of walls,
Amphitrite's destined halls,
Which her hoary sire now paves
With his blue and beaming waves.
Lo! the sun upsprings behind,
Broad, red, radiant, half-reclined
On the level quivering line
Of the waters crystalline;
And before that chasm of light,
As within a furnace bright,
Column, tower, and dome, and spire,
Shine like obelisks of fire,
Pointing with inconstant motion
From the altar of dark ocean
To the sapphire-tinted skies;
As the flames of sacrifice
From the marble shrines did rise,
As to pierce the dome of gold
Where Apollo spoke of old.

Sun-girt City, thou hast been
Ocean's child, and then his queen;
Now is come a darker day,
And thou soon must be his prey,
If the power that raised thee here
Hallow so thy watery bier.
A less drear ruin then than now,
With thy conquest-branded brow
Stooping to the slave of slaves
From thy throne, among the waves
Wilt thou be, when the sea-mew
Flies, as once before it flew,
O'er thine isles depopulate,

And all is in its ancient state,
Save where many a palace gate
With green sea-flowers overgrown
Like a rock of Ocean's own,
Topples o'er the abandoned sea
As the tides change sullenly.
The fisher on his watery way,
Wandering at the close of day,
Will spread his sail and seize his oar
Till he pass the gloomy shore,
Lest thy dead should, from their sleep
Bursting o'er the starlight deep,
Lead a rapid masque of death
O'er the waters of his path.

Those who alone thy towers behold
Quivering through aëreal gold,
As I now behold them here,
Would imagine not they were
Sepulchres, where human forms,
Like pollution-nourished worms,
To the corpse of greatness cling,
Murdered, and now mouldering:
But if Freedom should awake
In her omnipotence, and shake
From the Celtic Anarch's hold
All the keys of dungeons cold,
Where a hundred cities lie
Chained like thee, ingloriously,
Thou and all thy sister band
Might adorn this sunny land,
Twining memories of old time
With new virtues more sublime;
If not, perish thou and they! –

Clouds which stain truth's rising day
By her sun consumed away –
Earth can spare ye: while like flowers,
In the waste of years and hours,
From your dust new nations spring
With more kindly blossoming.

Perish – let there only be
Floating o'er thy heartless sea
As the garment of thy sky
Clothes the world immortally,
One remembrance, more sublime
Than the tattered pall of time,
Which scarce hides thy visage wan; –
That a tempest-cleaving Swan
Of the songs of Albion,
Driven from his ancestral streams
By the might of evil dreams,
Found a nest in thee; and Ocean
Welcomed him with such emotion
That its joy grew his, and sprung
From his lips like music flung
O'er a mighty thunder-fit,
Chastening terror: – what though yet
Poesy's unfailing River,
Which through Albion winds forever
Lashing with melodious wave
Many a sacred Poet's grave,
Mourn its latest nursling fled?
What though thou with all thy dead
Scarce can for this fame repay
Aught thine own? oh, rather say
Though thy sins and slaveries foul
Overcloud a sunlike soul?

As the ghost of Homer clings
Round Scamander's wasting springs;
As divinest Shakespeare's might
Fills Avon and the world with light
Like omniscient power which he
Imaged 'mid mortality;
As the love from Petrarch's urn,
Yet amid yon hills doth burn,
A quenchless lamp by which the heart
Sees things unearthly; – so thou art,
Mighty spirit – so shall be
The City that did refuge thee.

Lo, the sun floats up the sky
Like thought-wingèd Liberty,
Till the universal light
Seems to level plain and height;
From the sea a mist has spread,
And the beams of morn lie dead
On the towers of Venice now,
Like its glory long ago.
By the skirts of that gray cloud
Many-domèd Padua proud
Stands, a peopled solitude,
'Mid the harvest-shining plain,
Where the peasant heaps his grain
In the garner of his foe,
And the milk-white oxen slow
With the purple vintage strain,
Heaped upon the creaking wain,
That the brutal Celt may swill
Drunken sleep with savage will;
And the sickle to the sword
Lies unchanged, though many a lord,

Like a weed whose shade is poison,
Overgrows this region's foison,
Sheaves of whom are ripe to come
To destruction's harvest-home:
Men must reap the things they sow,
Force from force must ever flow,
Or worse; but 'tis a bitter woe
That love or reason cannot change
The despot's rage, the slave's revenge.
Padua, thou within whose walls
Those mute guests at festivals,
Son and Mother, Death and Sin,
Played at dice for Ezzelin,
Till Death cried, 'I win, I win!'
And Sin cursed to lose the wager,
But Death promised, to assuage her,
That he would petition for
Her to be made Vice-Emperor,
When the destined years were o'er,
Over all between the Po
And the eastern Alpine snow,
Under the mighty Austrian.
Sin smiled so as Sin only can,
And since that time, ay, long before
Both have ruled from shore to shore, –
That incestuous pair, who follow
Tyrants as the sun the swallow,
As Repentance follows Crime,
And as changes follow Time.

In thine halls the lamp of learning,
Padua, now no more is burning;
Like a meteor, whose wild way
Is lost over the grave of day,

It gleams betrayed and to betray:
Once remotest nations came
To adore that sacred flame,
When it lit not many a hearth
On this cold and gloomy earth:
Now new fires from antique light
Spring beneath the wide world's might;
But their spark lies dead in thee,
Trampled out by Tyranny.
As the Norway woodman quells,
In the depth of piny dells,
One light flame among the brakes,
While the boundless forest shakes,
And its mighty trunks are torn
By the fire thus lowly born:
The spark beneath his feet is dead,
He starts to see the flames it fed
Howling through the darkened sky
With a myriad tongues victoriously,
And sinks down in fear: so thou,
O Tyranny, beholdest now
Light around thee, and thou hearest
The loud flames ascend, and fearest:
Grovel on the earth; ay, hide
In the dust thy purple pride!

Noon descends around me now:
'Tis the noon of autumn's glow,
When a soft and purple mist
Like a vaporous amethyst,
Or an air-dissolvèd star
Mingling light and fragrance, far
From the curved horizon's bound
To the point of Heaven's profound,

Fills the overflowing sky;
And the plains that silent lie
Underneath, the leaves unsodden
Where the infant Frost has trodden
With his morning-wingèd feet,
Whose bright print is gleaming yet;
And the red and golden vines
Piercing with their trellised lines
The rough, dark-skirted wilderness;
The dun and bladed grass no less,
Pointing from this hoary tower
In the windless air; the flower
Glimmering at my feet; the line
Of the olive-sandalled Apennine
In the south dimly islanded;
And the Alps, whose snows are spread
High between the clouds and sun;
And of living things each one;
And my spirit which so long
Darkened this swift stream of song, –
Interpenetrated lie
By the glory of the sky:
Be it love, light, harmony,
Odour, or the soul of all
Which from Heaven like dew doth fall,
Or the mind which feeds this verse
Peopling the lone universe.

Noon descends, and after noon
Autumn's evening meets me soon,
Leading the infantine moon,
And that one star, which to her
Almost seems to minister

Half the crimson light she brings
From the sunset's radiant springs:
And the soft dreams of the morn
(Which like wingèd winds had borne
To that silent isle, which lies
Mid remembered agonies,
The frail bark of this lone being)
Pass, to other sufferers fleeing,
And its ancient pilot, Pain,
Sits beside the helm again.

Other flowering isles must be
In the sea of Life and Agony:
Other spirits float and flee
O'er that gulf: even now, perhaps,
On some rock the wild wave wraps,
With folded wings they waiting sit
For my bark, to pilot it
To some calm and blooming cove,
Where for me, and those I love,
May a windless bower be built,
Far from passion, pain, and guilt,
In a dell mid lawny hills,
Which the wild sea-murmur fills,
And soft sunshine, and the sound
Of old forests echoing round,
And the light and smell divine
Of all flowers that breathe and shine:
We may live so happy there,
That the Spirits of the Air,
Envying us, may even entice
To our healing Paradise
The polluting multitude;
But their rage would be subdued

By that clime divine and calm,
And the winds whose wings rain balm
On the uplifted soul, and leaves
Under which the bright sea heaves;
While each breathless interval
In their whisperings musical
The inspired soul supplies
With its own deep melodies,
And the love which heals all strife
Circling, like the breath of life,
All things in that sweet abode
With its own mild brotherhood:
They, not it, would change; and soon
Every sprite beneath the moon
Would repent its envy vain,
And the earth grow young again.

INVOCATION TO MISERY

I

Come, be happy! – sit near me,
Shadow-vested Misery:
Coy, unwilling, silent bride,
Mourning in thy robe of pride,
Desolation – deified!

II

Come, be happy! – sit near me:
Sad as I may seem to thee,
I am happier far than thou,
Lady, whose imperial brow
Is endiademed with woe.

III

Misery! we have known each other,
Like a sister and a brother
Living in the same lone home,
Many years – we must live some
Hours or ages yet to come.

IV

'Tis an evil lot, and yet
Let us make the best of it;
If love can live when pleasure dies,
We two will love, till in our eyes
This heart's Hell seem Paradise.

V

Come, be happy! – lie thee down
On the fresh grass newly mown,
Where the Grasshopper doth sing
Merrily – one joyous thing
In a world of sorrowing!

VI

There our tent shall be the willow,
And mine arm shall be thy pillow;
Sounds and odours, sorrowful
Because they once were sweet, shall lull
Us to slumber, deep and dull.

VII

Ha! thy frozen pulses flutter
With a love thou darest not utter.
Thou art murmuring – thou art weeping –
Is thine icy bosom leaping
While my burning heart lies sleeping?

VIII

Kiss me; – oh! thy lips are cold:
Round my neck thine arms enfold –
They are soft, but chill and dead;
And thy tears upon my head
Burn like points of frozen lead.

IX

Hasten to the bridal bed –
Underneath the grave 'tis spread:
In darkness may our love be hid,
Oblivion be our coverlid –
We may rest, and none forbid.

X

Clasp me till our hearts be grown
Like two shadows into one;
Till this dreadful transport may
Like a vapour fade away,
In the sleep that lasts alway.

XI

We may dream, in that long sleep,
That we are not those who weep;
E'en as Pleasure dreams of thee,
Life-deserting Misery,
Thou mayst dream of her with me.

XII

Let us laugh, and make our mirth,
At the shadows of the earth,
As dogs bay the moonlight clouds,
Which, like spectres wrapped in shrouds,
Pass o'er night in multitudes.

XIII

All the wide world, beside us,
Show like multitudinous
Puppets passing from a scene;
What but mockery can they mean,
Where I am – where thou hast been?

From JULIAN AND MADDALO

I RODE one evening with Count Maddalo
Upon the bank of land which breaks the flow
Of Adria towards Venice: a bare strand
Of hillocks, heaped from ever-shifting sand,
Matted with thistles and amphibious weeds,
Such as from earth's embrace the salt ooze breeds,
Is this; an uninhabited sea-side,
Which the lone fisher, when his nets are dried,
Abandons; and no other object breaks
The waste, but one dwarf tree and some few stakes
Broken and unrepaired, and the tide makes
A narrow space of level sand thereon,
Where 'twas our wont to ride while day went down.
This ride was my delight. I love all waste
And solitary places; where we taste
The pleasure of believing what we see
Is boundless, as we wish our souls to be:
And such was this wide ocean, and this shore
More barren than its billows; and yet more
Than all, with a remembered friend I love
To ride as then I rode; – for the winds drove
The living spray along the sunny air
Into our faces; the blue heavens were bare,
Stripped to their depths by the awakening north;
And, from the waves, sound like delight broke forth
Harmonizing with solitude, and sent
Into our hearts aëreal merriment.
So, as we rode, we talked; and the swift thought,
Winging itself with laughter, lingered not,
But flew from brain to brain, – such glee was ours,
Charged with light memories of remembered hours,

None slow enough for sadness: till we came
Homeward, which always makes the spirit tame.
This day had been cheerful but cold, and now
The sun was sinking, and the wind also.
Our talk grew somewhat serious, as may be
Talk interrupted with such raillery
As mocks itself, because it cannot scorn
The thoughts it would extinguish: — 'twas forlorn,
Yet pleasing, such as once, so poets tell,
The devils held within the dales of Hell
Concerning God, freewill and destiny:
Of all that earth has been or yet may be,
All that vain men imagine or believe,
Or hope can paint or suffering may achieve,
We descanted, and I (for ever still
Is it not wise to make the best of ill?)
Argued against despondency, but pride
Made my companion take the darker side.
The sense that he was greater than his kind
Had struck, methinks, his eagle spirit blind
By gazing on its own exceeding light.
Meanwhile the sun passed ere it should alight,
Over the horizon of the mountains; — Oh,
How beautiful is sunset, when the glow
Of Heaven descends upon a land like thee,
Thou Paradise of exiles, Italy!
Thy mountains, seas, and vineyards, and the towers
Of cities they encircle! — it was ours
To stand on thee, beholding it: and then,
Just where we had dismounted, the Count's men
Were waiting for us with the gondola. —
As those who pause on some delightful way
Though bent on pleasant pilgrimage, we stood
Looking upon the evening, and the flood

Which lay between the city and the shore,
Paved with the image of the sky ... the hoar
And aëry Alps towards the North appeared
Through mist, an heaven-sustaining bulwark reared
Between the East and West; and half the sky
Was roofed with clouds of rich emblazonry
Dark purple at the zenith, which still grew
Down the steep West into a wondrous hue
Brighter than burning gold, even to the rent
Where the swift sun yet paused in his descent
Among the many-folded hills: they were
Those famous Euganean hills, which bear,
As seen from Lido thro' the harbour piles,
The likeness of a lump of peakèd isles –
And then – as if the Earth and Sea had been
Dissolved into one lake of fire, were seen
Those mountains towering as from waves of flame
Around the vaporous sun, from which there came
The inmost purple spirit of light, and made
Their very peaks transparent.

STANZAS

I

THE sun is warm, the sky is clear,
  The waves are dancing fast and bright,
Blue isles and snowy mountains wear
  The purple noon's transparent might,
  The breath of the moist earth is light,
Around its unexpanded buds;
  Like many a voice of one delight,
The winds, the birds, the ocean floods,
The City's voice itself, is soft like Solitude's.

II

I see the Deep's untrampled floor
  With green and purple seaweeds strown;
I see the waves upon the shore,
  Like light dissolved in star-showers, thrown:
  I sit upon the sands alone, –
The lightning of the noontide ocean
  Is flashing round me, and a tone
Arises from its measured motion,
How sweet! did any heart now share in my emotion.

III

Alas! I have not hope nor health,
  Nor peace within nor calm around,
Nor that content surpassing wealth
  The sage in meditation found,
  And walked with inward glory crowned –

Nor fame, nor power, nor love, nor leisure.
   Others I see whom these surround –
Smiling they live, and call life pleasure; –
To me that cup has been dealt in another measure.

IV

Yet now despair itself is mild,
   Even as the winds and waters are;
I could lie down like a tired child,
   And weep away the life of care
   Which I have borne and yet must bear,
Till death like sleep might steal on me,
   And I might feel in the warm air
My cheek grow cold, and hear the sea
Breathe o'er my dying brain its last monotony.

V

Some might lament that I were cold,
   As I, when this sweet day is gone,
Which my lost heart, too soon grown old,
   Insults with this untimely moan;
   They might lament – for I am one
Whom men love not, – and yet regret,
   Unlike this day, which, when the sun
   Shall on its stainless glory set,
Will linger, though enjoyed, like joy in memory yet.

SONNET

Lift not the painted veil which those who live
Call Life: though unreal shapes be pictured there,
And it but mimic all we would believe
With colours idly spread, – behind, lurk Fear
And Hope, twin Destinies; who ever weave
Their shadows, o'er the chasm, sightless and drear.
I knew one who had lifted it – he sought,
For his lost heart was tender, things to love,
But found them not, alas! nor was there aught
The world contains, the which he could approve.
Through the unheeding many he did move,
A splendour among shadows, a bright blot
Upon this gloomy scene, a Spirit that strove
For truth, and like the Preacher found it not.

SONNET: ENGLAND IN 1819

An old, mad, blind, despised, and dying king, –
Princes, the dregs of their dull race, who flow
Through public scorn, – mud from a muddy spring, –
Rulers who neither see, nor feel, nor know,
But leech-like to their fainting country cling,
Till they drop, blind in blood, without a blow, –
A people starved and stabbed in the untilled field, –
An army, which liberticide and prey
Makes as a two-edged sword to all who wield, –
Golden and sanguine laws which tempt and slay;
Religion Christless, Godless – a book sealed;
A Senate, – Time's worst statute unrepealed, –
Are graves, from which a glorious Phantom may
Burst, to illumine our tempestuous day.

From PROMETHEUS UNBOUND

ACT I

CHORUS OF SPIRITS

FROM unremembered ages we
Gentle guides and guardians be
Of heaven-oppressed mortality;
And we breathe, and sicken not,
The atmosphere of human thought:
Be it dim, and dank, and gray,
Like a storm-extinguished day,
Travelled o'er by dying gleams;
  Be it bright as all between
Cloudless skies and windless streams,
  Silent, liquid, and serene;
As the birds within the wind,
  As the fish within the wave,
As the thoughts of man's own mind
  Float through all above the grave;
We make there our liquid lair,
Voyaging cloudlike and unpent
Through the boundless element:
Thence we bear the prophecy
Which begins and ends in thee!

FIRST SPIRIT

On a battle-trumpet's blast
I fled hither, fast, fast, fast,
'Mid the darkness upward cast.
From the dust of creeds outworn,
From the tyrant's banner torn,
Gathering 'round me, onward borne,

There was mingled many a cry –
Freedom! Hope! Death! Victory!
Till they faded through the sky;
And one sound, above, around,
One sound beneath, around, above,
Was moving; 'twas the soul of Love;
'Twas the hope, the prophecy,
Which begins and ends in thee.

SECOND SPIRIT

A rainbow's arch stood on the sea,
Which rocked beneath, immovably;
And the triumphant storm did flee,
Like a conqueror, swift and proud,
Between, with many a captive cloud,
A shapeless, dark and rapid crowd,
Each by lightning riven in half:
I heard the thunder hoarsely laugh:
Mighty fleets were strewn like chaff
And spread beneath a hell of death
O'er the white waters. I alit
On a great ship lightning-split,
And speeded hither on the sigh
Of one who gave an enemy
His plank, then plunged aside to die.

THIRD SPIRIT

I sate beside a sage's bed,
And the lamp was burning red
Near the book where he had fed,
When a Dream with plumes of flame,
To his pillow hovering came,
And I knew it was the same

Which had kindled long ago
Pity, eloquence, and woe;
And the world awhile below
Wore the shade, its lustre made.
It has borne me here as fleet
As Desire's lightning feet:
I must ride it back ere morrow,
Or the sage will wake in sorrow.

FOURTH SPIRIT

On a poet's lips I slept
Dreaming like a love-adept
In the sound his breathing kept;
Nor seeks nor finds he mortal blisses,
But feeds on the aëreal kisses
Of shapes that haunt thought's wildernesses.
He will watch from dawn to gloom
The lake-reflected sun illume
The yellow bees in the ivy-bloom,
Nor heed nor see, what things they be;
But from these create he can
Forms more real than living man,
Nurslings of immortality!
One of these awakened me,
And I sped to succour thee.

ACT II
SCENE I

Morning. A lovely Vale in the Indian Caucasus. ASIA *alone.*

ASIA. From all the blasts of heaven thou hast descended:
Yes, like a spirit, like a thought, which makes
Unwonted tears throng to the horny eyes,
And beatings haunt the desolated heart,
Which should have learnt repose: thou hast descended

Cradled in tempests; thou dost wake, O Spring!
O child of many winds! As suddenly
Thou comest as the memory of a dream,
Which now is sad because it hath been sweet;
Like genius, or like joy which riseth up
As from the earth, clothing with golden clouds
The desert of our life.
This is the season, this the day, the hour;
At sunrise thou shouldst come, sweet sister mine,
Too long desired, too long delaying, come!
How like death-worms the wingless moments crawl!
The point of one white star is quivering still
Deep in the orange light of widening morn
Beyond the purple mountains: through a chasm
Of wind-divided mist the darker lake
Reflects it: now it wanes: it gleams again
As the waves fade, and as the burning threads
Of woven cloud unravel in pale air:
'Tis lost! and through yon peaks of cloud-like snow
The roseate sunlight quivers: hear I not
The Aeolian music of her sea-green plumes
Winnowing the crimson dawn?

Scene II

A Forest, intermingled with Rocks and Caverns. ASIA *and*
PANTHEA *pass into it. Two young Fauns are sitting on a
Rock listening.*

SEMICHORUS I OF SPIRITS

The path through which that lovely twain
    Have passed, by cedar, pine, and yew.
    And each dark tree that ever grew,
    Is curtained out from Heaven's wide blue;
Nor sun, nor moon, nor wind, nor rain,
    Can pierce its interwoven bowers,

Nor aught, save where some cloud of dew,
Drifted along the earth-creeping breeze,
Between the trunks of the hoar trees,
    Hangs each a pearl in the pale flowers
  Of the green laurel, blown anew;
And bends, and then fades silently,
One frail and fair anemone:
Or when some star of many a one
That climbs and wanders through steep night,
Has found the cleft through which alone
Beams fall from high those depths upon
Ere it is borne away, away,
By the swift Heavens that cannot stay,
It scatters drops of golden light,
Like lines of rain that ne'er unite:
And the gloom divine is all around,
And underneath is the mossy ground.

SEMICHORUS II

There the voluptuous nightingales,
  Are awake through all the broad noonday.
When one with bliss or sadness fails,
    And through the windless ivy-boughs,
  Sick with sweet love, droops dying away
On its mate's music-panting bosom;
Another from the swinging blossom,
    Watching to catch the languid close
  Of the last strain, then lifts on high
  The wings of the weak melody,
'Till some new strain of feeling bear
  The song, and all the woods are mute;
When there is heard through the dim air
The rush of wings, and rising there
  Like many a lake-surrounded flute,

Sounds overflow the listener's brain
So sweet, that joy is almost pain.

Scene III

Song of Spirits

To the deep, to the deep,
        Down, down!
Through the shade of sleep,
Through the cloudy strife
Of Death and of Life;
Through the veil and the bar
Of things which seem and are
Even to the steps of the remotest throne,
        Down, down!

While the sound whirls around,
        Down, down!
As the fawn draws the hound,
As the lightning the vapour,
As a weak moth the taper;
Death, despair; love, sorrow;
Time both; to-day, to-morrow;
As steel obeys the spirit of the stone,
        Down, down!

Through the gray, void abysm,
        Down, down!
Where the air is no prism,
And the moon and stars are not,
And the cavern-crags wear not
The radiance of Heaven,
Nor the gloom to Earth given,
Where there is One pervading, One alone,
        Down, down!

In the depth of the deep,
   Down, down!
Like veiled lightning asleep,
Like the spark nursed in embers,
The last look Love remembers,
Like a diamond, which shines
On the dark wealth of mines,
A spell is treasured but for thee alone.
   Down, down!

We have bound thee, we guide thee;
   Down, down!
With the bright form beside thee;
Resist not the weakness,
Such strength is in meekness
That the Eternal, the Immortal,
Must unloose through life's portal
The snake-like Doom coiled underneath his throne
   By that alone.

Scene IV

ASIA. Who reigns? There was the Heaven and Earth at
 first,
And Light and Love; then Saturn, from whose throne
Time fell, an envious shadow: such the state
Of the earth's primal spirits beneath his sway,
As the calm joy of flowers and living leaves
Before the wind or sun has withered them
And semivital worms; but he refused
The birthright of their being, knowledge, power,
The skill which wields the elements, the thought
Which pierces this dim universe like light,
Self-empire, and the majesty of love;

For thirst of which they fainted. Then Prometheus
Gave wisdom, which is strength, to Jupiter,
And with this law alone, 'Let man be free,'
Clothed him with the dominion of wide Heaven.
To know nor faith, nor love, nor law; to be
Omnipotent but friendless is to reign;
And Jove now reigned; for on the race of man
First famine, and then toil, and then disease,
Strife, wounds, and ghastly death unseen before,
Fell; and the unseasonable seasons drove
With alternating shafts of frost and fire,
Their shelterless, pale tribes to mountain caves:
And in their desert hearts fierce wants he sent,
And mad disquietudes, and shadows idle
Of unreal good, which levied mutual war,
So ruining the lair wherein they raged.
Prometheus saw, and waked the legioned hopes
Which sleep within folded Elysian flowers,
Nepenthe, Moly, Amaranth, fadeless blooms,
That they might hide with thin and rainbow wings
The shape of Death; and Love he sent to bind
The disunited tendrils of that vine
Which bears the wine of life, the human heart;
And he tamed fire which, like some beast of prey,
Most terrible, but lovely, played beneath
The frown of man; and tortured to his will
Iron and gold, the slaves and signs of power,
And gems and poisons, and all subtlest forms
Hidden beneath the mountains and the waves.
He gave man speech, and speech created thought,
Which is the measure of the universe;
And Science struck the thrones of earth and heaven,
Which shook, but fell not; and the harmonious mind
Poured itself forth in all-prophetic song;

And music lifted up the listening spirit
Until it walked, exempt from mortal care,
Godlike, o'er the clear billows of sweet sound;
And human hands first mimicked and then mocked,
With moulded limbs more lovely than its own,
The human form, till marble grew divine;
And mothers, gazing, drank the love men see
Reflected in their race, behold, and perish.
He told the hidden power of herbs and springs,
And Disease drank and slept. Death grew like sleep.
He taught the implicated orbits woven
Of the wide-wandering stars; and how the sun
Changes his lair, and by what secret spell
The pale moon is transformed, when her broad eye
Gazes not on the interlunar sea:
He taught to rule, as life directs the limbs,
The tempest-wingèd chariots of the Ocean,
And the Celt knew the Indian. Cities then
Were built, and through their snow-like columns flowed
The warm winds, and the azure aether shone,
And the blue sea and shadowy hills were seen.
Such, the alleviations of his state,
Prometheus gave to man, for which he hangs
Withering in destined pain: but who rains down
Evil, the immedicable plague, which, while
Man looks on his creation like a God
And sees that it is glorious, drives him on,
The wreck of his own will, the scorn of earth,
The outcast, the abandoned, the alone?
Not Jove: while yet his frown shook Heaven, ay, when
His adversary from adamantine chains
Cursed him, he trembled like a slave. Declare
Who is his master? Is he too a slave?

SPIRIT

My coursers are fed with the lightning,
　　They drink of the whirlwind's stream,
And when the red morning is bright'ning
　　They bathe in the fresh sunbeam;
　　They have strength for their swiftness I deem,
Then ascend with me, daughter of Ocean.

I desire: and their speed makes night kindle;
　　I fear: they outstrip the Typhoon;
Ere the cloud piled on Atlas can dwindle
　　We encircle the earth and the moon:
　　We shall rest from long labours at noon:
Then ascend with me, daughter of Ocean.

SCENE V

PANTHEA. How thou art changed! I dare not look on thee;
I feel but see thee not. I scarce endure
The radiance of thy beauty. Some good change
Is working in the elements, which suffer
Thy presence thus unveiled. The Nereids tell
That on the day when the clear hyaline
Was cloven at thine uprise, and thou didst stand
Within a veinèd shell, which floated on
Over the calm floor of the crystal sea,
Among the Aegean isles, and by the shores
Which bear thy name; love, like the atmosphere
Of the sun's fire filling the living world,
Burst from thee, and illumined earth and heaven
And the deep ocean and the sunless caves
And all that dwells within them; till grief cast
Eclipse upon the soul from which it came:
Such art thou now; nor is it I alone,

Thy sister, thy companion, thine own chosen one,
But the whole world which seeks thy sympathy.
Hearest thou not sounds i' the air which speak the love
Of all articulate beings? Feelest thou not
The inanimate winds enamoured of thee? List!

[*Music.*

ASIA. Thy words are sweeter than aught else but his
Whose echoes they are: yet all love is sweet,
Given or returned. Common as light is love,
And its familiar voice wearies not ever.
Like the wide heaven, the all-sustaining air,
It makes the reptile equal to the God:
They who inspire it most are fortunate,
As I am now; but those who feel it most
Are happier still, after long sufferings,
As I shall soon become.

PANTHEA.   List! Spirits speak.

VOICE IN THE AIR, SINGING.

Life of Life! thy lips enkindle
    With their love the breath between them;
And thy smiles before they dwindle
    Make the cold air fire; then screen them
In those looks, where whoso gazes
Faints, entangled in their mazes.

Child of Light! thy limbs are burning
    Through the vest which seems to hide them;
As the radiant lines of morning
    Through the clouds ere they divide them;
And this atmosphere divinest
Shrouds thee wheresoe'er thou shinest.

Fair are others; none beholds thee,
  But thy voice sounds low and tender
Like the fairest, for it folds thee
  From the sight, that liquid splendour,
And all feel, yet see thee never,
As I feel now, lost for ever!

Lamp of Earth! where'er thou movest
  Its dim shapes are clad with brightness,
And the souls of whom thou lovest
  Walk upon the winds with lightness,
Till they fail, as I am failing,
Dizzy, lost, yet unbewailing!

ASIA

My soul is an enchanted boat,
  Which, like a sleeping swan, doth float
Upon the silver waves of thy sweet singing;
  And thine doth like an angel sit
  Beside a helm conducting it,
Whilst all the winds with melody are ringing.
  It seems to float ever, for ever,
  Upon that many-winding river,
  Between mountains, woods, abysses,
  A paradise of wildernesses!
  Till, like one in slumber bound,
Borne to the ocean, I float down, around,
Into a sea profound, of ever-spreading sound:

    Meanwhile thy spirit lifts its pinions
    In music's most serene dominions;
Catching the winds that fan that happy heaven.
    And we sail on, away, afar,
    Without a course, without a star,
But, by the instinct of sweet music driven;

Till through Elysian garden islets
By thee, most beautiful of pilots,
Where never mortal pinnace glided,
The boat of my desire is guided:
Realms where the air we breathe is love,
Which in the winds and on the waves doth move,
Harmonizing this earth with what we feel above.

We have passed Age's icy caves,
And Manhood's dark and tossing waves,
And Youth's smooth ocean, smiling to betray:
Beyond the glassy gulfs we flee
Of shadow-peopled Infancy,
Through Death and Birth, to a diviner day;
A paradise of vaulted bowers,
Lit by downward-gazing flowers,
And watery paths that wind between
Wildernesses calm and green,
Peopled by shapes too bright to see,
And rest, having beheld; somewhat like thee;
Which walk upon the sea, and chant melodiously!

ACT III

Scene III

PROMETHEUS.   Asia, thou light of life,
Shadow of beauty unbeheld: and ye,
Fair sister nymphs, who made long years of pain
Sweet to remember, through your love and care:
Henceforth we will not part. There is a cave,
All overgrown with trailing odorous plants,
Which curtain out the day with leaves and flowers,

And paved with veinèd emerald, and a fountain
Leaps in the midst with an awakening sound.
From its curved roof the mountain's frozen tears
Like snow, or silver, or long diamond spires,
Hang downward, raining forth a doubtful light:
And there is heard the ever-moving air,
Whispering without from tree to tree, and birds,
And bees; and all around are mossy seats,
And the rough walls are clothed with long soft grass;
A simple dwelling, which shall be our own;
Where we will sit and talk of time and change,
As the world ebbs and flows, ourselves unchanged.
What can hide man from mutability?
And if ye sigh, then I will smile; and thou,
Ione, shalt chant fragments of sea-music,
Until I weep, when ye shall smile away
The tears she brought, which yet were sweet to shed.
We will entangle buds and flowers and beams
Which twinkle on the fountain's brim, and make
Strange combinations out of common things,
Like human babes in their brief innocence;
And we will search, with looks and words of love,
For hidden thoughts, each lovelier than the last,
Our unexhausted spirits; and like lutes
Touched by the skill of the enamoured wind,
Weave harmonies divine, yet ever new,
From difference sweet where discord cannot be;
And hither come, sped on the charmèd winds,
Which meet from all the points of heaven, as bees
From every flower aëreal Enna feeds,
At their known island-homes in Himera,
The echoes of the human world, which tell
Of the low voice of love, almost unheard,
And dove-eyed pity's murmured pain, and music,

Itself the echo of the heart, and all
That tempers or improves man's life, now free;
And lovely apparitions, – dim at first,
Then radiant, as the mind, arising bright
From the embrace of beauty (whence the forms
Of which these are the phantoms) casts on them
The gathered rays which are reality –
Shall visit us, the progeny immortal
Of Painting, Sculpture, and rapt Poesy,
And arts, though unimagined, yet to be.
The wandering voices and the shadows these
Of all that man becomes, the mediators
Of that best worship love, by him and us
Given and returned; swift shapes and sounds, which
   grow
More fair and soft as man grows wise and kind,
And, veil by veil, evil and error fall:
Such virtue has the cave and place around.

       [*Turning to the* SPIRIT OF THE HOUR

For thee, fair Spirit, one toil remains. Ione,
Give her that curvèd shell, which Proteus old
Made Asia's nuptial boon, breathing within it
A voice to be accomplished, and which thou
Didst hide in grass under the hollow rock.

IONE. Thou most desired Hour, more loved and lovely
Than all thy sisters, this is the mystic shell;
See the pale azure fading into silver
Lining it with a soft yet glowing light:
Looks it not like lulled music sleeping there?

SPIRIT. It seems in truth the fairest shell of Ocean:
Its sound must be at once both sweet and strange.

PROMETHEUS. Go, borne over the cities of mankind
On whirlwind-footed coursers: once again
Outspeed the sun around the orbèd world;

And as thy chariot cleaves the kindling air,
Thou breathe into the many-folded shell,
Loosening its mighty music; it shall be
As thunder mingled with clear echoes: then
Return; and thou shalt dwell beside our cave.
And thou, O, Mother Earth! —

THE EARTH.   I hear, I feel;
Thy lips are on me, and their touch runs down
Even to the adamantine central gloom
Along these marble nerves; 'tis life, 'tis joy,
And through my withered, old, and icy frame
The warmth of an immortal youth shoots down
Circling. Henceforth the many children fair
Folded in my sustaining arms; all plants,
And creeping forms, and insects rainbow-winged,
And birds, and beasts, and fish, and human shapes,
Which drew disease and pain from my wan bosom,
Draining the poison of despair, shall take
And interchange sweet nutriment; to me
Shall they become like sister-antelopes
By one fair dam, snow-white and swift as wind,
Nursed among lilies near a brimming stream.
The dew-mists of my sunless sleep shall float
Under the stars like balm: night-folded flowers
Shall suck unwithering hues in their repose:
And men and beasts in happy dreams shall gather
Strength for the coming day, and all its joy:
And death shall be the last embrace of her
Who takes the life she gave, even as a mother
Folding her child, says, 'Leave me not again.'

ASIA. Oh, mother! wherefore speak the name of death?
Cease they to love, and move, and breathe, and
    speak,
Who die?

THE EARTH. It would avail not to reply:
  Thou art immortal, and this tongue is known
  But to the uncommunicating dead.
  Death is the veil which those who live call life:
  They sleep, and it is lifted: and meanwhile
  In mild variety the seasons mild
  With rainbow-skirted showers, and odorous winds,
  And long blue meteors cleansing the dull night,
  And the life-kindling shafts of the keen sun's
  All-piercing bow, and the dew-mingled rain
  Of the calm moonbeams, a soft influence mild,
  Shall clothe the forests and the fields, ay, even
  The crag-built deserts of the barren deep,
  With ever-living leaves, and fruits, and flowers.
  And thou! There is a cavern where my spirit
  Was panted forth in anguish whilst thy pain
  Made my heart mad, and those who did inhale it
  Became mad too, and built a temple there,
  And spoke, and were oracular, and lured
  The erring nations round to mutual war,
  And faithless faith, such as Jove kept with thee;
  Which breath now rises, as amongst tall weeds
  A violet's exhalation, and it fills
  With a serener light and crimson air
  Intense, yet soft, the rocks and woods around;
  It feeds the quick growth of the serpent vine,
  And the dark linkèd ivy tangling wild,
  And budding, blown, or odour-faded blooms
  Which star the winds with points of coloured light,
  As they rain through them, and bright golden globes
  Of fruit, suspended in their own green heaven,
  And through their veinèd leaves and amber stems
  The flowers whose purple and translucid bowls
  Stand ever mantling with aëreal dew,

The drink of spirits: and it circles round,
Like the soft waving wings of noonday dreams,
Inspiring calm and happy thoughts, like mine,
Now thou art thus restored. This cave is thine.
Arise! Appear!
    [*A Spirit rises in the likeness of a winged child.*

Scene IV

PANTHEA.   It is the delicate spirit
That guides the earth through heaven. From afar
The populous constellations call that light
The loveliest of the planets; and sometimes
It floats along the spray of the salt sea,
Or makes its chariot of a foggy cloud,
Or walks through fields or cities while men sleep,
Or o'er the mountain tops, or down the rivers,
Or through the green waste wilderness, as now,
Wondering at all it sees. Before Jove reigned
It loved our sister Asia, and it came
Each leisure hour to drink the liquid light
Out of her eyes, for which it said it thirsted
As one bit by a dipsas, and with her
It made its childish confidence, and told her
All it had known or seen, for it saw much,
Yet idly reasoned what it saw; and called her –
For whence it sprung it knew not, nor do I –

ACT IV

IONE. I see a chariot like that thinnest boat,
In which the Mother of the Months is borne
By ebbing light into her western cave,
When she upsprings from interlunar dreams;
O'er which is curved an orblike canopy

Of gentle darkness, and the hills and woods,
Distinctly seen through that dusk aery veil,
Regard like shapes in an enchanter's glass;
Its wheels are solid clouds, azure and gold,
Such as the genii of the thunderstorm
Pile on the floor of the illumined sea
When the sun rushes under it; they roll
And move and grow as with an inward wind;
Within it sits a wingèd infant, white
Its countenance, like the whiteness of bright snow,
Its plumes are as feathers of sunny frost,
Its limbs gleam white, through the wind-flowing folds
Of its white robe, woof of ethereal pearl.
Its hair is white, the brightness of white light
Scattered in strings; yet its two eyes are heavens
Of liquid darkness, which the Deity
Within seems pouring, as a storm is poured
From jaggèd clouds, out of their arrowy lashes,
Tempering the cold and radiant air around,
With fire that is not brightness; in its hand
It sways a quivering moonbeam, from whose point
A guiding power directs the chariot's prow
Over its wheelèd clouds, which as they roll
Over the grass, and flowers, and waves, wake sounds,
Sweet as a singing rain of silver dew.

.   .   .

The Earth

It interpenetrates my granite mass,
  Through tangled roots and trodden clay doth pass
Into the utmost leaves and delicatest flowers;
  Upon the winds, among the clouds 'tis spread,
  It wakes a life in the forgotten dead,
They breathe a spirit up from their obscurest bowers.

And like a storm bursting its cloudy prison
With thunder, and with whirlwind, has arisen
Out of the lampless caves or unimagined being:
With earthquake shock and swiftness making shiver
Thought's stagnant chaos, unremoved for ever,
Till hate, and fear, and pain, light-vanquished shadows,
fleeing,

Leave Man, who was a many-sided mirror,
Which could distort to many a shape of error,
This true fair world of things, a sea reflecting love;
Which over all his kind, as the sun's heaven
Gliding o'er ocean, smooth, serene, and even,
Darting from starry depths radiance and life, doth move:

Leave Man, even as a leprous child is left,
Who follows a sick beast to some warm cleft
Of rocks, through which the might of healing springs is
poured;
Then when it wanders home with rosy smile,
Unconscious, and its mother fears awhile
It is a spirit, then, weeps on her child restored.

Man, oh, not men! a chain of linkèd thought,
Of love and might to be divided not,
Compelling the elements with adamantine stress;
As the sun rules, even with a tyrant's gaze,
The unquiet republic of the maze
Of planets, struggling fierce towards heaven's free wilder-
ness.

Man, one harmonious soul of many a soul,
Whose nature is its own divine control,
Where all things flow to all, as rivers to the sea;

Familiar acts are beautiful through love;
　Labour, and pain, and grief, in life's green grove
Sport like tame beasts, none knew how gentle they could
　　be!

His will, with all mean passions, bad delights,
　And selfish cares, its trembling satellites,
A spirit ill to guide, but mighty to obey,
　Is as a tempest-wingèd ship, whose helm
　Love rules, through waves which dare not overwhelm,
Forcing life's wildest shores to own its sovereign sway.

All things confess his strength. Through the cold mass
　Of marble and of colour his dreams pass;
Bright threads whence mothers weave the robes their child-
　　ren wear;
　Language is a perpetual Orphic song,
　Which rules with Daedal harmony a throng
Of thoughts and forms, which else senseless and shapeless
　　were.

The lightning is his slave; heaven's utmost deep
　Gives up her stars, and like a flock of sheep
They pass before his eye, are numbered, and roll on!
　The tempest is his steed, he strides the air;
　And the abyss shouts from her depth laid bare,
Heaven, hast thou secrets? Man unveils me; I have none.

· · · · ·

Demogorgon

This is the day, which down the void abysm
　At the Earth-born's spell yawns for Heaven's despotism,
　　And Conquest is dragged captive through the deep:
Love, from its awful throne of patient power

154

In the wise heart, from the last giddy hour
  Of dread endurance, from the slippery, steep,
And narrow verge of crag-like agony, springs
And folds over the world its healing wings.

Gentleness, Virtue, Wisdom, and Endurance,
These are the seals of that most firm assurance
  Which bars the pit over Destruction's strength;
And if, with infirm hand, Eternity,
Mother of many acts and hours, should free
  The serpent that would clasp her with his length;
These are the spells by which to reassume
An empire o'er the disentangled doom.

To suffer woes which Hope thinks infinite;
To forgive wrongs darker than death or night;
  To defy Power, which seems omnipotent;
To love, and bear; to hope till Hope creates
From his own wreck the thing it contemplates;
  Neither to change, nor falter, nor repent;
This, like thy glory, Titan, is to be
Good, great and joyous, beautiful and free;
This is alone Life, Joy, Empire, and Victory.

From THE CENCI

ACT III

SCENE I

BEATRICE.   How comes this hair undone?
Its wandering strings must be what blind me so,
And yet I tied it fast. – O, horrible!
The pavement sinks under my feet! The walls
Spin round! I see a woman weeping there,
And standing calm and motionless, whilst I
Slide giddily as the world reels. . . . My God!
The beautiful blue heaven is flecked with blood!
The sunshine on the floor is black! The air
Is changed to vapours such as the dead breathe
In charnel pits! Pah! I am choked! There creeps
A clinging, black, contaminating mist
About me . . . 'tis substantial, heavy thick,
I cannot pluck it from me, for it glues
My fingers and my limbs to one another,
And eats into my sinews, and dissolves
My flesh to a pollution, poisoning
The subtle, pure, and inmost spirit of life!
My God! I never knew what the mad felt
Before; for I am mad beyond all doubt!
(*More wildly.*) No, I am dead! These putrefying limbs
Shut round and sepulchre the panting soul
Which would burst forth into the wandering air!
                               (*A pause.*)
What hideous thought was that I had even now?
'Tis gone; and yet its burthen remains here
O'er these dull eyes . . . upon this weary heart!
O, world! O, life! O, day! O, misery!

ACT V

SCENE IV

GIACOMO. Know you not, Mother . . . Sister, know you
  not?
  Bernardo even now is gone to implore
  The Pope to grant our pardon.

LUCRETIA.   Child, perhaps
  It will be granted. We may all then live
  To make these woes a tale for distant years:
  Oh, what a thought! It gushes to my heart
  Like the warm blood.

BEATRICE.   Yet both will soon be cold.
  Oh, trample out that thought! Worse than despair,
  Worse than the bitterness of death, is hope:
  It is the only ill which can find place
  Upon the giddy, sharp and narrow hour
  Tottering beneath us. Plead with the swift frost
  That it should spare the eldest flower of spring:
  Plead with awakening earthquake, o'er whose couch
  Even now a city stands, strong, fair, and free;
  Now stench and blackness yawn, like death. Oh, plead
  With famine, or wind-walking Pestilence,
  Blind lightning, or the deaf sea, not with man!
  Cruel, cold, formal man; righteous in words,
  In deeds a Cain. No, Mother, we must die:
  Since such is the reward of innocent lives;
  Such the alleviation of worst wrongs.
  And whilst our murderers live, and hard, cold men,
  Smiling and slow, walk through a world of tears
  To death as to life's sleep; 'twere just the grave
  Were some strange joy for us. Come, obscure Death,
  And wind me in thine all-embracing arms!
  Like a fond mother hide me in thy bosom,

And rock me to the sleep from which none wake.
Live ye, who live, subject to one another
As we were once, who now . . .

BERNARDO rushes in

BERNARDO.   Oh, horrible!
That tears, that looks, that hope poured forth in prayer,
Even till the heart is vacant and despairs,
Should all be vain! The ministers of death
Are waiting round the doors. I thought I saw
Blood on the face of one . . . What if 'twere fancy?
Soon the heart's blood of all I love on earth
Will sprinkle him, and he will wipe it off
As if 'twere only rain. O life! O world!
Cover me! let me be no more! To see
That perfect mirror of pure innocence
Wherein I gazed, and grew happy and good,
Shivered to dust! To see thee, Beatrice,
Who made all lovely thou didst look upon . . .
Thee, light of life . . . dead, dark! while I say, sister,
To hear I have no sister; and thou, Mother,
Whose love was as a bond to all our loves . . .
Dead! The sweet bond broken!

Enter CAMILLO and GUARDS

                                  They come! Let me
Kiss those warm lips before their crimson leaves
Are blighted . . . white . . . cold. Say farewell, before
Death chokes that gentle voice! Oh, let me hear
You speak!

BEATRICE. Farewell, my tender brother. Think
Of our sad fate with gentleness, as now:
And let mild, pitying thoughts lighten for thee
Thy sorrow's load. Err not in harsh despair,
But tears and patience. One thing more, my child:
For thine own sake be constant to the love

Thou bearest us; and to the faith that I,
Though wrapped in a strange cloud of crime and shame,
Lived ever holy and unstained. And though
Ill tongues shall wound me, and our common name
Be as a mark stamped on thine innocent brow
For men to point at as they pass, do thou
Forbear, and never think a thought unkind
Of those, who perhaps love thee in their graves.
So mayest thou die as I do; fear and pain
Being subdued. Farewell! Farewell! Farewell!

BERNARDO. I cannot say farewell!

CAMILLO.   Oh, Lady Beatrice!

BEATRICE. Give yourself no unnecessary pain,
My dear Lord Cardinal. Here, Mother, tie
My girdle for me, and bind up this hair
In any simple knot; ay, that does well.
And yours I see is coming down. How often
Have we done this for one another; now
We shall not do it any more. My Lord,
We are quite ready. Well, 'tis very well.

ODE TO THE WEST WIND

I

O WILD West Wind, thou breath of Autumn's being,
Thou, from whose unseen presence the leaves dead
Are driven, like ghosts from an enchanter fleeing,

Yellow, and black, and pale, and hectic red,
Pestilence-stricken multitudes: O thou,
Who chariotest to their dark wintry bed

The wingèd seeds, where they lie cold and low,
Each like a corpse within its grave, until
Thine azure sister of the Spring shall blow

Her clarion o'er the dreaming earth, and fill
(Driving sweet buds like flocks to feed in air)
With living hues and odours plain and hill:

Wild Spirit, which art moving everywhere;
Destroyer and preserver; hear, oh, hear!

II

Thou on whose stream, mid the deep sky's commotion,
Loose clouds like earth's decaying leaves are shed,
Shook from the tangled boughs of Heaven and Ocean,

Angels of rain and lightning: there are spread
On the blue surface of thine aëry surge,
Like the bright hair uplifted from the head

Of some fierce Maenad, even from the dim verge
Of the horizon to the zenith's height,
The locks of the approaching storm. Thou dirge

Of the dying year, to which this closing night
Will be the dome of a vast sepulchre,
Vaulted with all thy congregated might

Of vapours, from whose solid atmosphere
Black rain, and fire, and hail will burst: oh, hear!

III

Thou who didst waken from his summer dreams
The blue Mediterranean, where he lay,
Lulled by the coil of his crystalline streams,

Beside a pumice isle in Baiae's bay,
And saw in sleep old palaces and towers
Quivering within the wave's intenser day,

All overgrown with azure moss and flowers
So sweet, the sense faints picturing them! Thou
For whose path the Atlantic's level powers

Cleave themselves into chasms, while far below
The sea-blooms and the oozy woods which wear
The sapless foliage of the ocean, know

Thy voice, and suddenly grow gray with fear,
And tremble and despoil themselves: oh, hear!

IV

If I were a dead leaf thou mightest bear;
If I were a swift cloud to fly with thee;
A wave to pant beneath thy power, and share

The impulse of thy strength, only less free
Than thou, O uncontrollable! If even
I were as in my boyhood, and could be

The comrade of thy wanderings over Heaven,
As then, when to outstrip thy skiey speed
Scarce seemed a vision; I would ne'er have striven

As thus with thee in prayer in my sore need.
Oh, lift me as a wave, a leaf, a cloud!
I fall upon the thorns of life! I bleed!

A heavy weight of hours has chained and bowed
One too like thee: tameless, and swift, and proud.

v

Make me thy lyre, even as the forest is:
What if my leaves are falling like its own!
The tumult of thy mighty harmonies

Will take from both a deep, autumnal tone,
Sweet though in sadness. Be thou, Spirit fierce,
My spirit! Be thou me, impetuous one!

Drive my dead thoughts over the universe
Like withered leaves to quicken a new birth!
And, by the incantation of this verse,

Scatter, as from an unextinguished hearth
Ashes and sparks, my words among mankind!
Be through my lips to unawakened earth

The trumpet of a prophecy! O, Wind,
If Winter comes, can Spring be far behind?

AN EXHORTATION

CHAMELEONS feed on light and air:
  Poets' food is love and fame:
If in this wide world of care
  Poets could but find the same
With as little toil as they,
  Would they ever change their hue
  As the light chameleons do,
Suiting it to every ray
    Twenty times a day?

Poets are on this cold earth,
  As chameleons might be,
Hidden from their early birth
  In a cave beneath the sea;
Where light is, chameleons change:
  Where love is not, poets do:
  Fame is love disguised: if few
Find either, never think it strange
    That poets range.

Yet dare not stain with wealth or power
  A poet's free and heavenly mind:
If bright chameleons should devour
  Any food but beams and wind,
They would grow as earthly soon
  As their brother lizards are.
  Children of a sunnier star,
Spirits from beyond the moon,
    Oh, refuse the boon!

THE INDIAN SERENADE

I

I ARISE from dreams of thee
In the first sweet sleep of night.
When the winds are breathing low,
And the stars are shining bright:
I arise from dreams of thee,
And a spirit in my feet
Hath led me – who knows how?
To thy chamber window, Sweet!

II

The wandering airs they faint
On the dark, the silent stream –
The Champak odours fail
Like sweet thoughts in a dream;
The nightingale's complaint,
It dies upon her heart; –
As I must on thine,
Oh, belovèd as thou art!

III

Oh lift me from the grass!
I die! I faint! I fail!
Let thy love in kisses rain
On my lips and eyelids pale.
My cheek is cold and white, alas!
My heart beats loud and fast; –
Oh! press it to thine own again,
Where it will break at last.

TO SOPHIA (MISS STACEY)

I

Thou art fair, and few are fairer
  Of the nymphs of earth or ocean;
They are robes that fit the wearer –
  Those soft limbs of thine, whose motion
Ever falls and sifts and glances
As the life within them dances.

II

Thy deep eyes, a double Planet,
  Gaze the wisest into madness
With soft clear fire, – the winds that fan it
  Are those thoughts of tender gladness
Which, like zephyrs on the billow,
Make thy gentle soul their pillow.

III

If, whatever face thou paintest
  In those eyes, grows pale with pleasure,
If the fainting soul is faintest
  When it hears thy harp's wild measure,
Wonder not that when thou speakest
Of the weak my heart is weakest.

IV

As dew beneath the wind of morning,
  As the sea which whirlwinds waken,
As the birds at thunder's warning,
  As aught mute yet deeply shaken,
As one who feels an unseen spirit
Is my heart when thine is near it.

LOVE'S PHILOSOPHY

I

THE fountains mingle with the river
    And the rivers with the Ocean,
The winds of Heaven mix for ever
    With a sweet emotion;
Nothing in the world is single;
    All things by a law divine
In one spirit meet and mingle.
    Why not I with thine? –

II

See the mountains kiss high Heaven
    And the waves clasp one another;
No sister-flower would be forgiven
    If it disdained its brother;
And the sunlight clasps the earth
    And the moonbeams kiss the sea:
What is all this sweet work worth
    If thou kiss not me?

THE SENSITIVE PLANT

PART FIRST

A SENSITIVE Plant in a garden grew,
And the young winds fed it with silver dew,
And it opened its fan-like leaves to the light,
And closed them beneath the kisses of Night.

And the Spring arose on the garden fair,
Like the Spirit of Love felt everywhere;
And each flower and herb on Earth's dark breast
Rose from the dreams of its wintry rest.

But none ever trembled and panted with bliss
In the garden, the field, or the wilderness,
Like a doe in the noontide with love's sweet want,
As the companionless Sensitive Plant.

The snowdrop, and then the violet,
Arose from the ground with warm rain wet,
And their breath was mixed with fresh odour, sent
From the turf, like the voice and the instrument.

Then the pied wind-flowers and the tulip tall,
And narcissi, the fairest among them all,
Who gaze on their eyes in the stream's recess,
Till they die of their own dear loveliness;

And the Naiad-like lily of the vale,
Whom youth makes so fair and passion so pale
That the light of its tremulous bells is seen
Through their pavilions of tender green;

And the hyacinth purple, and white, and blue,
Which flung from its bells a sweet peal anew
Of music so delicate, soft, and intense,
It was felt like an odour within the sense;

And the rose like a nymph to the bath addressed,
Which unveiled the depth of her glowing breast,
Till, fold after fold, to the fainting air
The soul of her beauty and love lay bare:

And the wand-like lily, which lifted up,
As a Maenad, its moonlight-coloured cup,
Till the fiery star, which is its eye,
Gazed through clear dew on the tender sky;

And the jessamine faint, and the sweet tuberose,
The sweetest flower for scent that blows;
And all rare blossoms from every clime
Grew in that garden in perfect prime.

And on the stream whose inconstant bosom
Was pranked, under boughs of embowering blossom,
With golden and green light, slanting through
Their heaven of many a tangled hue,

Broad water-lilies lay tremulously,
And starry river-buds glimmered by,
And around them the soft stream did glide and dance
With a motion of sweet sound and radiance.

And the sinuous paths of lawn and of moss,
Which led through the garden along and across,
Some open at once to the sun and the breeze,
Some lost among bowers of blossoming trees,

Were all paved with daisies and delicate bells
As fair as the fabulous asphodels,
And flow'rets which, drooping as day drooped too,
Fell into pavilions, white, purple, and blue,
To roof the glow-worm from the evening dew.

And from this undefilèd Paradise
The flowers (as an infant's awakening eyes
Smile on its mother, whose singing sweet
Can first lull, and at last must awaken it),

When Heaven's blithe winds had unfolded them,
As mine-lamps enkindle a hidden gem,
Shone smiling to Heaven, and every one
Shared joy in the light of the gentle sun;

For each one was interpenetrated
With the light and the odour its neighbour shed,
Like young lovers whom youth and love make dear
Wrapped and filled by their mutual atmosphere.

But the Sensitive Plant which could give small fruit
Of the love which it felt from the leaf to the root,
Received more than all, it loved more than ever,
Where none wanted but it, could belong to the giver, –

For the Sensitive Plant has no bright flower;
Radiance and odour are not its dower;
It loves, even like Love, its deep heart is full,
It desires what it has not, the Beautiful!

The light winds which from unsustaining wings
Shed the music of many murmurings;
The beams which dart from many a star
Of the flowers whose hues they bear afar;

The plumèd insects swift and free,
Like golden boats on a sunny sea,
Laden with light and odour, which pass
Over the gleam of the living grass;

The unseen clouds of the dew, which lie
Like fire in the flowers till the sun rides high,
Then wander like spirits among the spheres,
Each cloud faint with the fragrance it bears;

The quivering vapours of dim noontide,
Which like a sea o'er the warm earth glide,
In which every sound, and odour, and beam,
Move, as reeds in a single stream;

Each and all like ministering angels were
For the Sensitive Plant sweet joy to bear,
Whilst the lagging hours of the day went by
Like windless clouds o'er a tender sky.

And when evening descended from Heaven above,
And the Earth was all rest, and the air was all love,
And delight, though less bright, was far more deep,
And the day's veil fell from the world of sleep,

And the beasts, and the birds, and the insects were
    drowned
In an ocean of dreams without a sound;
Whose waves never mark, though they ever impress
The light sand which paves it, consciousness;

(Only overhead the sweet nightingale
Ever sang more sweet as the day might fail,
And snatches of its Elysian chant
Were mixed with the dreams of the Sensitive Plant); –

The Sensitive Plant was the earliest
Upgathered into the bosom of rest;
A sweet child weary of its delight,
The feeblest and yet the favourite,
Cradled within the embrace of Night.

PART SECOND

There was a Power in this sweet place,
An Eve in this Eden; a ruling Grace
Which to the flowers, did they waken or dream,
Was as God is to the starry scheme.

A Lady, the wonder of her kind,
Whose form was upborne by a lovely mind
Which, dilating, had moulded her mien and motion
Like a sea-flower unfolded beneath the ocean,

Tended the garden from morn to even:
And the meteors of that sublunar Heaven,
Like the lamps of the air when Night walks forth,
Laughed round her footsteps up from the Earth!

She had no companion of mortal race,
But her tremulous breath and her flushing face
Told, whilst the morn kissed the sleep from her eyes,
That her dreams were less slumber than Paradise:

As if some bright Spirit for her sweet sake
Had deserted Heaven while the stars were awake,
As if yet around her he lingering were,
Though the veil of daylight concealed him from her.

Her step seemed to pity the grass it pressed;
You might hear by the heaving of her breast,
That the coming and going of the wind
Brought pleasure there and left passion behind.

And wherever her aëry footstep trod,
Her trailing hair from the grassy sod
Erased its light vestige, with shadowy sweep,
Like a sunny storm o'er the dark green deep.

I doubt not the flowers of that garden sweet
Rejoiced in the sound of her gentle feet;
I doubt not they felt the spirit that came
From her glowing fingers through all their frame.

She sprinkled bright water from the stream
On those that were faint with the sunny beam;
And out of the cups of the heavy flowers
She emptied the rain of the thunder-showers.

She lifted their heads with her tender hands,
And sustained them with rods and osier-bands;
If the flowers had been her own infants, she
Could never have nursed them more tenderly.

And all killing insects and gnawing worms,
And things of obscene and unlovely forms,
She bore, in a basket of Indian woof,
Into the rough woods far aloof, –

In a basket, of grasses and wild-flowers full,
The freshest her gentle hands could pull
For the poor banished insects, whose intent,
Although they did ill, was innocent.

But the bee and the beamlike ephemeris
Whose path is the lightning's, and soft moths that kiss
The sweet lips of the flowers, and harm not, did she
Make her attendant angels be.

And many an antenatal tomb,
Where butterflies dream of the life to come,
She left clinging round the smooth and dark
Edge of the odorous cedar bark.

This fairest creature from earliest Spring
Thus moved through the garden ministering
All the sweet season of Summertide,
And ere the first leaf looked brown – she died!

PART THIRD

Three days the flowers of the garden fair,
Like stars when the moon is awakened, were,
Or the waves of Baiae, ere luminous
She floats up through the smoke of Vesuvius.

And on the fourth, the Sensitive Plant
Felt the sound of the funeral chant,
And the steps of the bearers, heavy and slow,
And the sobs of the mourners, deep and low;

The weary sound and the heavy breath,
And the silent motions of passing death,
And the smell, cold, oppressive, and dank,
Sent through the pores of the coffin-plank;

The dark grass, and the flowers among the grass,
Were bright with tears as the crowd did pass;
From their sighs the wind caught a mournful tone,
And sate in the pines, and gave groan for groan.

The garden, once fair, became cold and foul,
Like the corpse of her who had been its soul,
Which at first was lovely as if in sleep,
Then slowly changed, till it grew a heap
To make men tremble who never weep.

Swift Summer into the Autumn flowed,
And frost in the mist of the morning rode,
Though the noonday sun looked clear and bright,
Mocking the spoil of the secret night.

The rose-leaves, like flakes of crimson snow,
Paved the turf and the moss below.
The lilies were drooping, and white, and wan,
Like the head and the skin of a dying man.

And Indian plants, of scent and hue
The sweetest that ever were fed on dew,
Leaf by leaf, day after day,
Were massed into the common clay.

And the leaves, brown, yellow, and gray, and red,
And white with the whiteness of what is dead,
Like troops of ghosts on the dry wind passed;
Their whistling noise made the birds aghast.

And the gusty winds waked the wingèd seeds,
Out of their birthplace of ugly weeds,
Till they clung round many a sweet flower's stem,
Which rotted into the earth with them.

The water-blooms under the rivulet
Fell from the stalks on which they were set;
And the eddies drove them here and there,
As the winds did those of the upper air.

Then the rain came down, and the broken stalks
Were bent and tangled across the walks;
And the leafless network of parasite bowers
Massed into ruin; and all sweet flowers.

Between the time of the wind and the snow
All loathliest weeds began to grow,
Whose coarse leaves were splashed with many a speck,
Like the water-snake's belly and the toad's back.

And thistles, and nettles, and darnels rank,
And the dock, and henbane, and hemlock dank,
Stretched out its long and hollow shank.
And stifled the air till the dead wind stank.

And plants, at whose names the verse feels loath,
Filled the place with a monstrous undergrowth,
Prickly, and pulpous, and blistering, and blue,
Livid, and starred with a lurid dew.

And agarics, and fungi, with mildew and mould
Started like mist from the wet ground cold;
Pale, fleshy, as if the decaying dead
With a spirit of growth had been animated!

Spawn, weeds, and filth, a leprous scum,
Made the running rivulet thick and dumb,
And at its outlet flags huge as stakes
Dammed it up with roots knotted like water-snakes.

And hour by hour, when the air was still,
The vapours arose which have strength to kill;
At morn they were seen, at noon they were felt,
At night they were darkness no star could melt.

And unctuous meteors from spray to spray
Crept and flitted in broad noonday
Unseen; every branch on which they alit
By a venomous blight was burned and bit.

The Sensitive Plant, like one forbid,
Wept, and the tears within each lid
Of its folded leaves, which together grew,
Were changed to a blight of frozen glue.

For the leaves soon fell, and the branches soon
By the heavy axe of the blast were hewn;
The sap shrank to the root through every pore
As blood to a heart that will beat no more.

For Winter came: the wind was his whip:
One choppy finger was on his lip:
He had torn the cataracts from the hills
And they clanked at his girdle like manacles;

His breath was a chain which without a sound
The earth, and the air, and the water bound;
He came, fiercely driven, in his chariot-throne
By the tenfold blasts of the Arctic zone.

Then the weeds which were forms of living death
Fled from the frost to the earth beneath.
Their decay and sudden flight from frost
Was but like the vanishing of a ghost!

And under the roots of the Sensitive Plant
The moles and the dormice died for want:
The birds dropped stiff from the frozen air
And were caught in the branches naked and bare.

First there came down a thawing rain
And its dull drops froze on the boughs again;
Then there steamed up a freezing dew
Which to the drops of the thaw-rain grew;

And a northern whirlwind, wandering about
Like a wolf that had smelt a dead child out,
Shook the boughs thus laden, and heavy, and stiff,
And snapped them off with his rigid griff.

When Winter had gone and Spring came back
The Sensitive Plant was a leafless wreck;
But the mandrakes, and toadstools, and docks, and
  darnels,
Rose like the dead from their ruined charnels.

CONCLUSION

Whether the Sensitive Plant, or that
Which within its boughs like a Spirit sat,
Ere its outward form had known decay,
Now felt this change, I cannot say.

Whether that Lady's gentle mind,
No longer with the form combined
Which scattered love, as stars do light,
Found sadness, where it left delight,

I dare not guess; but in this life
Of error, ignorance, and strife,
Where nothing is, but all things seem,
And we the shadows of the dream,

It is a modest creed, and yet
Pleasant if one considers it,
To own that death itself must be,
Like all the rest, a mockery.

That garden sweet, that lady fair,
And all sweet shapes and odours there,
In truth have never passed away:
'Tis we, 'tis ours, are changed; not they.

For love, and beauty, and delight,
There is no death nor change: their might
Exceeds our organs, which endure
No light, being themselves obscure.

THE CLOUD

I BRING fresh showers for the thirsting flowers,
    From the seas and the streams;
I bear light shade for the leaves when laid
    In their noonday dreams.
From my wings are shaken the dews that waken
    The sweet buds every one,
When rocked to rest on their mother's breast,
    As she dances about the sun.
I wield the flail of the lashing hail,
    And whiten the green plains under,
And then again I dissolve it in rain,
    And laugh as I pass in thunder.

I sift the snow on the mountains below,
    And their great pines groan aghast;
And all the night 'tis my pillow white,
    While I sleep in the arms of the blast.
Sublime on the towers of my skiey bowers,
    Lightning my pilot sits;
In a cavern under is fettered the thunder,
    It struggles and howls at fits;
Over earth and ocean, with gentle motion,
    This pilot is guiding me,
Lured by the love of the genii that move
    In the depths of the purple sea;
Over the rills, and the crags, and the hills,
    Over the lakes and the plains,
Wherever he dream, under mountain or stream,
    The Spirit he loves remains;
And I all the while bask in Heaven's blue smile,
    Whilst he is dissolving in rains.

The sanguine Sunrise, with his meteor eyes,
　　And his burning plumes outspread,
Leaps on the back of my sailing rack,
　　When the morning star shines dead:
As on the jag of a mountain crag,
　　Which an earthquake rocks and swings,
An eagle alit one moment may sit
　　In the light of its golden wings.
And when Sunset may breathe, from the lit sea beneath,
　　It ardours of rest and of love,
And the crimson pall of eve may fall
　　From the depth of Heaven above,
With wings folded I rest, on mine aëry nest,
　　As still as a brooding dove.

That orbèd maiden with white fire laden,
　　Whom mortals call the Moon,
Glides glimmering o'er my fleece-like floor,
　　By the midnight breezes strewn;
And wherever the beat of her unseen feet,
　　Which only the angels hear,
May have broken the woof of my tent's thin roof,
　　The stars peep behind her and peer;
And I laugh to see them whirl and flee,
　　Like a swarm of golden bees,
When I widen the rent in my wind-built tent,
　　Till the calm rivers, lakes, and seas,
Like strips of the sky fallen through me on high,
　　Are each paved with the moon and these.

I bind the Sun's throne with a burning zone,
　　And the Moon's with a girdle of pearl;
The volcanoes are dim, and the stars reel and swim,
　　When the whirlwinds my banner unfurl.

From cape to cape, with a bridge-like shape,
 Over a torrent sea,
Sunbeam-proof, I hang like a roof, –
 The mountains its columns be.
The triumphal arch through which I march
 With hurricane, fire, and snow,
When the Powers of the air are chained to my chair,
 Is the million-coloured bow;
The sphere-fire above its soft colours wove,
 While the moist Earth was laughing below.

I am the daughter of Earth and Water,
 And the nursling of the Sky;
I pass through the pores of the ocean and shores;
 I change, but I cannot die.
For after the rain when with never a stain
 The pavilion of Heaven is bare,
And the winds and sunbeams with their convex gleams
 Build up the blue dome of air,
I silently laugh at my own cenotaph,
 And out of the caverns of rain,
Like a child from the womb, like a ghost from the tomb,
 I arise and unbuild it again.

TO A SKYLARK

HAIL to thee, blithe Spirit!
   Bird thou never wert,
That from Heaven, or near it,
   Pourest thy full heart
In profuse strains of unpremeditated art.

Higher still and higher
   From the earth thou springest
Like a cloud of fire;
   The blue deep thou wingest,
And singing still dost soar, and soaring ever singest.

In the golden lightning
   Of the sunken sun,
O'er which clouds are bright'ning,
   Thou dost float and run;
Like an unbodied joy whose race is just begun.

The pale purple even
   Melts around thy flight;
Like a star of Heaven,
   In the broad daylight
Thou art unseen, but yet I hear thy shrill delight,

Keen as are the arrows
   Of that silver sphere,
Whose intense lamp narrows
   In the white dawn clear
Until we hardly see – we feel that it is there.

All the earth and air
   With thy voice is loud,
As, when night is bare,
   From one lonely cloud
The moon rains out her beams, and Heaven is over-
     flowed.

What thou art we know not;
   What is most like thee?
From rainbow clouds there flow not
   Drops so bright to see
As from thy presence showers a rain of melody.

Like a Poet hidden
   In the light of thought,
Singing hymns unbidden,
   Till the world is wrought
To sympathy with hopes and fears it heeded not:

Like a high-born maiden
   In a palace-tower,
Soothing her love-laden
   Soul in secret hour
With music sweet as love, which overflows her bower:

Like a glow-worm golden
   In a dell of dew,
Scattering unbeholden
   Its aëreal hue
Among the flowers and grass, which screen it from the
     view!

Like a rose embowered
   In its own green leaves,
By warm winds deflowered,
   Till the scent it gives
Makes faint with too much sweet those heavy-wingèd
     thieves:

Sound of vernal showers
   On the twinkling grass,
Rain-awakened flowers,
   All that ever was
Joyous, and clear, and fresh, thy music doth surpass:

Teach us, Sprite or Bird,
   What sweet thoughts are thine:
I have never heard
   Praise of love or wine
That panted forth a flood of rapture so divine.

Chorus Hymeneal,
   Or triumphal chant,
Matched with thine would be all
   But an empty vaunt,
A thing wherein we feel there is some hidden want.

What objects are the fountains
   Of thy happy strain?
What fields, or waves, or mountains?
   What shapes of sky or plain?
What love of thine own kind? what ignorance of pain?

With thy clear keen joyance
   Languor cannot be:
Shadow of annoyance
   Never came near thee:
Thou lovest – but ne'er knew love's sad satiety.

Waking or asleep,
  Thou of death must deem
Things more true and deep
  Than we mortals dream,
Or how could thy notes flow in such a crystal stream?

We look before and after,
  And pine for what is not:
Our sincerest laughter
  With some pain is fraught;
Our sweetest songs are those that tell of saddest thought.

Yet if we could scorn
  Hate, and pride, and fear;
If we were things born
  Not to shed a tear,
I know not how thy joy we ever should come near.

Better than all measures
  Of delightful sound,
Better than all treasures
  That in books are found,
Thy skill to poet were, thou scorner of the ground!

Teach me half the gladness
  That thy brain must know,
Such harmonious madness
  From my lips would flow
The world should listen then – as I am listening now.

LETTER TO MARIA GISBORNE

T H E spider spreads her webs, whether she be
In poet's tower, cellar, or barn, or tree;
The silk-worm in the dark green mulberry leaves
His winding sheet and cradle ever weaves;
So I, a thing whom moralists call worm,
Sit spinning still round this decaying form,
From the fine threads of rare and subtle thought –
No net of words in garish colours wrought
To catch the idle buzzers of the day –
But a soft cell, where when that fades away,
Memory may clothe in wings my living name
And feed it with the asphodels of fame,
Which in those hearts which must remember me
Grow, making love an immortality.

   Whoever should behold me now, I wist,
Would think I were a mighty mechanist,
Bent with sublime Archimedean art
To breathe a soul into the iron heart
Of some machine portentous, or strange gin,
Which by the force of figured spells might win
Its way over the sea, and sport therein;
For round the walls are hung dread engines, such
As Vulcan never wrought for Jove to clutch
Ixion or the Titan: – or the quick
Wit of that man of God, St Dominic,
To convince Atheist, Turk, or Heretic,
Or those in philanthropic council met,
Who thought to pay some interest for the debt
They owed to Jesus Christ for their salvation,
By giving a faint foretaste of damnation

To Shakespeare, Sidney, Spenser, and the rest
Who made our land an island of the blest,
When lamp-like Spain, who now relumes her fire
On Freedom's hearth, grew dim with Empire: –
With thumbscrews, wheels, with tooth and spike and
   jag,
Which fishers found under the utmost crag
Of Cornwall and the storm-encompassed isles,
Where to the sky the rude sea rarely smiles
Unless in treacherous wrath, as on the morn
When the exulting elements in scorn,
Satiated with destroyed destruction, lay
Sleeping in beauty on their mangled prey,
As panthers sleep; – and other strange and dread
Magical forms the brick floor overspread, –
Proteus transformed to metal did not make
More figures, or more strange; nor did he take
Such shapes of unintelligible brass,
Or heap himself in such a horrid mass
Of tin and iron not to be understood;
And forms of unimaginable wood,
To puzzle Tubal Cain and all his brood:
Great screws, and cones, and wheels, and groovèd blocks,
The elements of what will stand the shocks
Of wave and wind and time. – Upon the table
More knacks and quips there be than I am able
To catalogize in this verse of mine: –
A pretty bowl of wood – not full of wine,
But quicksilver; that dew which the gnomes drink
When at their subterranean toil they swink,
Pledging the demons of the earthquake, who
Reply to them in lava – cry halloo!
And call out to the cities o'er their head, –
Roofs, towers, and shrines, the dying and the dead,

Crash through the chinks of earth – and then all quaff
Another rouse, and hold their sides and laugh.
This quicksilver no gnome has drunk – within
The walnut bowl it lies, veinèd and thin,
In colour like the wake of light that stains
The Tuscan deep, when from the moist moon rains
The inmost shower of its white fire – the breeze
Is still – blue Heaven smiles over the pale seas.
And in this bowl of quicksilver – for I
Yield to the impulse of an infancy
Outlasting manhood – I have made to float
A rude idealism of a paper boat: –
A hollow screw with cogs – Henry will know
The thing I mean and laugh at me, – if so
He fears not I should do more mischief. – Next
Lie bills and calculations much perplexed,
With steam-boats, frigates, and machinery quaint
Traced over them in blue and yellow paint.
Then comes a range of mathematical
Instruments, for plans nautical and statical;
A heap of rosin, a queer broken glass
With ink in it; – a china cup that was
What it will never be again, I think, –
A thing from which sweet lips were wont to drink
The liquor doctors rail at – and which I
Will quaff in spite of them – and when we die
We'll toss up who died first of drinking tea,
And cry out, – 'Heads or tails?' where'er we be.
Near that a dusty paint-box, some odd hooks,
A half-burnt match, an ivory block, three books,
Where conic sections, spherics, logarithms,
To great Laplace, from Saunderson and Sims,
Lie heaped in their harmonious disarray
Of figures, – disentangle them who may.

Baron de Tott's Memoirs beside them lie,
And some odd volumes of old chemistry.
Near those a most inexplicable thing,
With lead in the middle – I'm conjecturing
How to make Henry understand; but no –
I'll leave, as Spenser says, with many mo,
This secret in the pregnant womb of time,
Too vast a matter for so weak a rhyme.

And here like some weird Archimage sit I,
Plotting dark spells, and devilish enginery,
The self-impelling steam-wheels of the mind
Which pump up oaths from clergymen, and grind
The gentle spirit of our meek reviews
Into a powdery foam of salt abuse,
Ruffling the ocean of their self-content; –
I sit – and smile or sigh as is my bent,
But not for them – Libeccio rushes round
With an inconstant and an idle sound,
I heed him more than them – the thunder-smoke
Is gathering on the mountains, like a cloak
Folded athwart their shoulders broad and bare;
The ripe corn under the undulating air
Undulates like an ocean; – and the vines
Are trembling wide in all their trellised lines –
The murmur of the awakening sea doth fill
The empty pauses of the blast; – the hill
Looks hoary through the white electric rain,
And from the glens beyond, in sullen strain,
The interrupted thunder howls; above
One chasm of Heaven smiles, like the eye of Love
On the unquiet world; – while such things are,
How could one worth your friendship heed the war
Of worms? the shriek of the world's carrion jays,
Their censure, or their wonder, or their praise?

You are not here! the quaint witch Memory sees,
In vacant chairs, your absent images,
And points where once you sat, and now should be
But are not, – I demand if ever we
Shall meet as then we met; – and she replies,
Veiling in awe her second-sighted eyes;
'I know the past alone – but summon home
My sister Hope, – she speaks of all to come.'
But I, an old diviner, who knew well
Every false verse of that sweet oracle,
Turned to the sad enchantress once again,
And sought a respite from my gentle pain,
In citing every passage o'er and o'er
Of our communion – how on the sea-shore
We watched the ocean and the sky together,
Under the roof of blue Italian weather;
How I ran home through last year's thunder-storm,
And felt the transverse lightning linger warm
Upon my cheek – and how we often made
Feasts for each other, where good will outweighed
The frugal luxury of our country cheer,
As well it might, were it less firm and clear
Than ours must ever be; – and how we spun
A shroud of talk to hide us from the sun
Of this familiar life, which seems to be
But is not: – or is but quaint mockery
Of all we would believe, and sadly blame
The jarring and inexplicable frame
Of this wrong world: – and then anatomize
The purposes and thoughts of men whose eyes
Were closed in distant years; – or widely guess
The issue of the earth's great business,
When we shall be as we no longer are –
Like babbling gossips safe, who hear the war

Of winds, and sigh, but tremble not; – or how
You listened to some interrupted flow
Of visionary rhyme, – in joy and pain
Struck from the inmost fountains of my brain,
With little skill perhaps; – or how we sought
Those deepest wells of passion or of thought
Wrought by wise poets in the waste of years,
Staining their sacred waters with our tears;
Quenching a thirst ever to be renewed!
Or how I, wisest lady! then endued
The language of a land which now is free,
And, winged with thoughts of truth and majesty,
Flits round the tyrant's sceptre like a cloud,
And bursts the peopled prisons, and cries aloud,
'My name is Legion!' – that majestic tongue
Which Calderon over the desert flung
Of ages and of nations; and which found
An echo in our hearts, and with the sound
Startled oblivion; – thou wert then to me
As is a nurse – when inarticulately
A child would talk as its grown parents do.
If living winds the rapid clouds pursue,
If hawks chase doves through the aethereal way,
Huntsmen the innocent deer, and beasts their prey,
Why should not we rouse with the spirit's blast
Out of the forest of the pathless past
These recollected pleasures?
                                    You are now
In London, that great sea, whose ebb and flow
At once is deaf and loud, and on the shore
Vomits its wrecks, and still howls on for more.
Yet in its depth what treasures! You will see
That which was Godwin, – greater none than he
Though fallen – and fallen on evil times – to stand

Among the spirits of our age and land,
Before the dread tribunal of *to come*
The foremost, – while Rebuke cowers pale and dumb.
You will see Coleridge – he who sits obscure
In the exceeding lustre and the pure
Intense irradiation of a mind,
Which, with its own internal lightning blind,
Flags wearily through darkness and despair –
A cloud-encircled meteor of the air,
A hooded eagle among blinking owls. –
You will see Hunt – one of those happy souls
Which are the salt of the earth, and without whom
This world would smell like what it is – a tomb;
Who is, what others seem; his room no doubt
Is still adorned with many a cast from Shout,
With graceful flowers tastefully placed about;
And coronals of bay from ribbons hung,
And brighter wreaths in neat disorder flung;
The gifts of the most learned among some dozens
Of female friends, sisters-in-law, and cousins.
And there is he with his eternal puns,
Which beat the dullest brain for smiles, like duns
Thundering for money at a poet's door;
Alas! it is no use to say, 'I'm poor!'
Or oft in graver mood, when he will look
Things wiser than were ever read in book,
Except in Shakespeare's wisest tenderness. –
You will see Hogg, – and I cannot express
His virtues, – though I know that they are great,
Because he locks, then barricades the gate
Within which they inhabit; – of his wit
And wisdom, you'll cry out when you are bit.
He is a pearl within an oyster shell,

192

One of the richest of the deep; – and there
Is English Peacock, with his mountain Fair,
Turned into a Flamingo; – that shy bird
That gleams i' the Indian air – have you not heard
When a man marries, dies, or turns Hindoo,
His best friends hear no more of him? – but you
Will see him, and will like him too, I hope,
With the milk-white Snowdonian Antelope
Matched with this cameleopard – his fine wit
Makes such a wound, the knife is lost in it;
A strain too learnèd for a shallow age,
Too wise for selfish bigots; let his page,
Which charms the chosen spirits of the time,
Fold itself up for the serener clime
Of years to come, and find its recompense
In that just expectation. – Wit and sense,
Virtue and human knowledge; all that might
Make this dull world a business of delight,
Are all combined in Horace Smith. – And these,
With some exceptions, which I need not tease
Your patience by descanting on, – are all
You and I know in London.
                              I recall
My thoughts, and bid you look upon the night.
As water does a sponge, so the moonlight
Fills the void, hollow, universal air –
What see you? – unpavilioned Heaven is fair,
Whether the moon, into her chamber gone,
Leaves midnight to the golden stars, or wan
Climbs with diminished beams the azure steep;
Or whether clouds sail o'er the inverse deep,
Piloted by the many-wandering blast,
And the rare stars rush through them dim and fast: –

All this is beautiful in every land. –
But what see you beside? – a shabby stand
Of Hackney coaches – a brick house or wall
Fencing some lonely court, white with the scrawl
Of our unhappy politics; – or worse –
A wretched woman reeling by, whose curse
Mixed with the watchman's partner of her trade,
You must accept in place of serenade –
Or yellow-haired Pollonia murmuring
To Henry, some unutterable thing.
I see a chaos of green leaves and fruit
Built round dark caverns, even to the root
Of the living stems that feed them – in whose bowers
There sleep in their dark dew the folded flowers;
Beyond, the surface of the unsickled corn
Trembles not in the slumbering air, and borne
In circles quaint, and ever-changing dance,
Like wingèd stars the fire-flies flash and glance,
Pale in the open moonshine, but each one
Under the dark trees seems a little sun,
A meteor tamed; a fixed star gone astray
From the silver regions of the milky way; –
Afar the Contadino's song is heard,
Rude, but made sweet by distance – and a bird
Which cannot be the Nightingale, and yet
I know none else that sings so sweet as it
At this late hour; – and then all is still –
Now – Italy or London, which you will!

Next winter you must pass with me; I'll have
My house by that time turned into a grave
Of dead despondence and low-thoughted care,
And all the dreams which our tormentors are;

Oh, that Hunt, Hogg, Peacock, and Smith were there,
With everything belonging to them fair! –
We will have books, Spanish, Italian, Greek;
And ask one week to make another week
As like his father, as I'm unlike mine,
Which is not his fault, as you may divine.
Though we eat little flesh and drink no wine,
Yet let's be merry: we'll have tea and toast;
Custards for supper, and an endless host
Of syllabubs and jellies and mince-pies,
And other such lady-like luxuries, –
Feasting on which we will philosophize!
And we'll have fires out of the Grand Duke's wood,
To thaw the six weeks' winter in our blood.
And then we'll talk; – what shall we talk about?
Oh! there are themes enough for many a bout
Of thought-entangled descant; – as to nerves –
With cones and parallelograms and curves
I've sworn to strangle them if once they dare
To bother me – when you are with me there.
And they shall never more sip laudanum,
From Helicon or Himeros; – well, come,
And in despite of God and of the devil,
We'll make our friendly philosophic revel
Outlast the leafless time; till buds and flowers
Warn the obscure inevitable hours,
Sweet meeting by sad parting to renew; –
'To-morrow to fresh woods and pastures new.'

From THE WITCH OF ATLAS

V

A LOVELY lady garmented in light
   From her own beauty – deep her eyes, as are
Two openings of unfathomable night
   Seen through a Temple's cloven roof – her hair
Dark – the dim brain whirls dizzy with delight,
   Picturing her form; her soft smiles shone afar,
And her low voice was heard like love, and drew
All living things towards this wonder new.

VI

And first the spotted cameleopard came,
   And then the wise and fearless elephant;
Then the sly serpent, in the golden flame
   Of his own volumes intervolved; – all gaunt
And sanguine beasts her gentle looks made tame.
   They drank before her at her sacred fount;
And every beast of beating heart grew bold,
Such gentleness and power even to behold.

VII

The brinded lioness led forth her young,
   That she might teach them how they should forgo
Their inborn thirst of death; the pard unstrung
   His sinews at her feet, and sought to know
With looks whose motions spoke without a tongue
   How he might be as gentle as the doe.
The magic circle of her voice and eyes
All savage natures did imparadise.

VIII

And old Silenus, shaking a green stick
   Of lilies, and the wood-gods in a crew
Came, blithe, as in the olive copses thick
   Cicadae are, drunk with the noonday dew:
And Dryope and Faunus followed quick,
   Teasing the God to sing them something new;
Till in this case they found the lady lone,
Sitting upon a seat of emerald stone.

IX

And universal Pan, 'tis said, was there,
   And though none saw him, – through the adamant
Of the deep mountains, through the trackless air,
   And through those living spirits, like a want,
He passed out of his everlasting lair
   Where the quick heart of the great world doth pant,
And felt that wondrous lady all alone, –
And she felt him, upon her emerald throne.

X

And every nymph of stream and spreading tree,
   And every shepherdess of Ocean's flocks,
Who drives her white waves over the green sea,
   And Ocean with the brine on his gray locks,
And quaint Priapus with his company,
   All came, much wondering how the enwombèd rocks
Could have brought forth so beautiful a birth; –
Her love subdued their wonder and their mirth.

XI

The herdsmen and the mountain maidens came,
   And the rude kings of pastoral Garamant –
Their spirits shook within them, as a flame

Stirred by the air under a cavern gaunt:
Pigmies, and Polyphemes, by many a name,
  Centaurs, and Satyrs, and such shapes as haunt
Wet clefts, – and lumps neither alive nor dead,
Dog-headed, bosom-eyed, and bird-footed.

XII

For she was beautiful – her beauty made
  The bright world dim, and everything beside
Seemed like the fleeting image of a shade:
  No thought of living spirit could abide,
Which to her looks had ever been betrayed,
  On any object in the world so wide,
On any hope within the circling skies,
But on her form, and in her inmost eyes.

ODE TO LIBERTY

I

A GLORIOUS people vibrated again
    The lightning of the nations: Liberty
From heart to heart, from tower to tower, o'er Spain,
    Scattering contagious fire into the sky,
Gleamed. My soul spurned the chains of its dismay,
        And in the rapid plumes of song
        Clothed itself, sublime and strong,
(As a young eagle soars the morning clouds among,)
    Hovering in verse o'er its accustomed prey;
        Till from its station in the Heaven of fame
    The Spirit's whirlwind rapped it, and the ray
        Of the remotest sphere of living flame
Which paves the void was from behind it flung,
    As foam from a ship's swiftness, when there came
    A voice out of the deep: I will record the same.

II

The Sun and the serenest Moon sprang forth:
    The burning stars of the abyss were hurled
Into the depths of Heaven. The daedal earth,
    That island in the ocean of the world,
Hung in its cloud of all-sustaining air:
        But this divinest universe
        Was yet a chaos and a curse,
For thou wert not: but, power from worst producing worse,
    The spirit of the beasts was kindled there,
        And of the birds, and of the watery forms,
    And there was war among them, and despair
        Within them, raging without truce or terms:
The bosom of their violated nurse

Groaned, for beasts warred on beasts, and worms on
    worms,
And men on men; each heart was as a hell of storms.

III

Man, the imperial shape, then multiplied
    His generations under the pavilion
Of the Sun's throne: palace and pyramid,
    Temple and prison, to many a swarming million
Were, as to mountain-wolves their raggèd caves.
        This human living multitude
        Was savage, cunning, blind, and rude,
For thou wert not; but o'er the populous solitude,
    Like one fierce cloud over a waste of waves,
        Hung Tyranny; beneath, sate deified
The sister-pest, congregator of slaves;
        Into the shadow of her pinions wide
Anarchs and priests, who feed on gold and blood
    Till with the stain their inmost souls are dyed,
    Drove the astonished herds of men from every side.

IV

The nodding promontories, and blue isles,
    And cloud-like mountains, and dividuous waves
Of Greece, basked glorious in the open smiles
    Of favouring Heaven: from their enchanted caves
Prophetic echoes flung dim melody.
        On the unapprehensive wild
        The vine, the corn, the olive mild,
Grew savage yet, to human use unreconciled;
    And, like unfolded flowers beneath the sea,
        Like the man's thought dark in the infant's brain,
    Like aught that is which wraps what is to be,
        Art's deathless dreams lay veiled by many a vein

Of Parian stone; and, yet a speechless child,
  Verse murmured, and Philosophy did strain
  His lidless eyes for thee; when o'er the Aegean main

V

Athens arose: a city such as vision
  Builds from the purple crags and silver towers
Of battlemented cloud, as in derision
  Of kingliest masonry: the ocean-floors
Pave it; the evening sky pavilions it;
      Its portals are inhabited
      By thunder-zonèd winds, each head
Within its cloudy wings with sun-fire garlanded, –
  A divine work! Athens, diviner yet,
    Gleamed with its crest of columns, on the will
  Of man, as on a mount of diamond, set;
    For thou wert, and thine all-creative skill
Peopled, with forms that mock the eternal dead
  In marble immortality, that hill
  Which was thine earliest throne and latest oracle.

VI

Within the surface of Time's fleeting river
  Its wrinkled image lies, as then it lay
Immovably unquiet, and for ever
  It trembles, but it cannot pass away!
The voices of thy bards and sages thunder
      With an earth-awakening blast
      Through the caverns of the past:
(Religion veils her eyes; Oppression shrinks aghast:)
  A wingèd sound of joy, and love, and wonder,
    Which soars where Expectation never flew,
  Rending the veil of space and time asunder!
    One ocean feeds the clouds, and streams, and dew;

One Sun illumines Heaven; one Spirit vast
　With life and love makes chaos ever new,
　As Athens doth the world with thy delight renew.

VII

Then Rome was, and from thy deep bosom fairest,
　Like a wolf-cub from a Cadmaean Maenad,
She drew the milk of greatness, though thy dearest
　From that Elysian food was yet unweanèd;
And many a deed of terrible uprightness
　　　By thy sweet love was sanctified;
　　　And in thy smile, and by thy side,
Saintly Camillus lived, and firm Atilius died.
　But when tears stained thy robe of vestal whiteness,
　　　And gold profaned thy Capitolian throne,
　Thou didst desert, with spirit-wingèd lightness,
　　　The senate of the tyrants: they sunk prone
Slaves of one tyrant: Palatinus sighed
　　Faint echoes of Ionian song; that tone
　　Thou didst delay to hear, lamenting to disown.

VIII

From what Hyrcanian glen or frozen hill,
　Or piny promontory of the Arctic main,
Or utmost islet inaccessible,
　Didst thou lament the ruin of thy reign,
Teaching the woods and waves, and desert rocks,
　　　And every Naiad's ice-cold urn,
　　　To talk in echoes sad and stern
Of that sublimest lore which man had dared unlearn?
　For neither didst thou watch the wizard flocks
　　Of the Scald's dreams, nor haunt the Druid's sleep.
　What if the tears rained through thy shattered locks
　　Were quickly dried? for thou didst groan, not weep,

When from its sea of death, to kill and burn,
  The Galilean serpent forth did creep,
  And made thy world an undistinguishable heap.

IX

A thousand years the Earth cried, 'Where art thou?'
  And then the shadow of thy coming fell
On Saxon Alfred's olive-cinctured brow:
  And many a warrior-peopled citadel.
Like rocks which fire lifts out of the flat deep,
     Arose in sacred Italy,
     Frowning o'er the tempestuous sea
Of kings, and priests, and slaves, in tower-crowned
    majesty;
  That multitudinous anarchy did sweep
    And burst around their walls, like idle foam,
  Whilst from the human spirit's deepest deep
    Strange melody with love and awe struck dumb
Dissonant arms; and Art, which cannot die,
  With divine wand traced on our earthly home
  Fit imagery to pave Heaven's everlasting dome.

X

Thou huntress swifter than the Moon! thou terror
  Of the world's wolves! thou bearer of the quiver,
Whose sunlike shafts pierce tempest-wingèd Error,
  As light may pierce the clouds when they dissever
In the calm regions of the orient day!
     Luther caught thy wakening glance;
     Like lightning, from his leaden lance
Reflected, it dissolved the visions of the trance
  In which, as in a tomb, the nations lay;
    And England's prophets hailed thee as their queen,
  In songs whose music cannot pass away,
    Though it must flow forever: not unseen

Before the spirit-sighted countenance
  Of Milton didst thou pass, from the sad scene
  Beyond whose night he saw, with a dejected mien.

XI

The eager hours and unreluctant years
  As on a dawn-illumined mountain stood,
Trampling to silence their loud hopes and fears,
  Darkening each other with their multitude,
And cried aloud, 'Liberty!' Indignation
      Answered Pity from her cave;
      Death grew pale within the grave,
And Desolation howled to the destroyer, Save!
  When like Heaven's Sun girt by the exhalation
    Of its own glorious light, thou didst arise,
  Chasing thy foes from nation unto nation
    Like shadows: as if day had cloven the skies
At dreaming midnight o'er the western wave,
  Men started, staggering with a glad surprise,
  Under the lightnings of thine unfamiliar eyes.

XII

Thou Heaven of earth! what spells could pall thee then
  In ominous eclipse? a thousand years
Bred from the slime of deep Oppression's den,
  Dyed all thy liquid light with blood and tears,
Till thy sweet stars could weep the stain away;
      How like Bacchanals of blood
      Round France, the ghastly vintage, stood
Destruction's sceptred slaves, and Folly's mitred brood!
  When one, like them, but mightier far than they,
    The Anarch of thine own bewildered powers,
  Rose: armies mingled in obscure array,
    Like clouds with clouds, darkening the sacred bowers

Of serene Heaven. He, by the past pursued,
  Rests with those dead, but unforgotten hours,
  Whose ghosts scare victor kings in their ancestral
    towers.

XIII

England yet sleeps: was she not called of old?
  Spain calls her now, as with its thrilling thunder
Vesuvius wakens Aetna, and the cold
  Snow-crags by its reply are cloven in sunder:
O'er the lit waves every Aeolian isle
        From Pithecusa to Pelorus
        Howls, and leaps, and glares in chorus:
They cry, 'Be dim; ye lamps of Heaven suspended o'er us!'
  Her chains are threads of gold, she need but smile
    And they dissolve; but Spain's were links of steel,
    Till bit to dust by virtue's keenest file.
      Twins of a single destiny! appeal
To the eternal years enthroned before us
  In the dim West; impress us from a seal,
  All ye have thought and done! Time cannot dare conceal.

XIV

Tomb of Arminius! render up thy dead
  Till, like a standard from a watch-tower's staff,
His soul may stream over the tyrant's head;
  Thy victory shall be his epitaph,
Wild Bacchanal of truth's mysterious wine,
        King-deluded Germany,
        His dead spirit lives in thee.
Why do we fear or hope? thou art already free!
  And thou, lost Paradise of this divine
    And glorious world! thou flowery wilderness!
    Thou island of eternity! thou shrine
      Where Desolation, clothed with loveliness,

Worships the thing thou wert! O Italy,
  Gather thy blood into thy heart; repress
  The beasts who make their dens thy sacred palaces.

XV

Oh, that the free would stamp the impious name
  Of KING into the dust! or write it there,
So that this blot upon the page of fame
  Were as a serpent's path, which the light air
Erases, and the flat sands close behind!
      Ye the oracle have heard:
      Lift the victory-flashing sword,
And cut the snaky knots of this foul gordian word,
  Which, weak itself as stubble, yet can bind
    Into a mass, irrefragably firm,
  The axes and the rods which awe mankind;
    The sound has poison in it, 'tis the sperm
Of what makes life foul, cankerous, and abhorred;
  Disdain not thou, at thine appointed term,
  To set thine armèd heel on this reluctant worm.

XVI

Oh, that the wise from their bright minds would kindle
  Such lamps within the dome of this dim world,
That the pale name of PRIEST might shrink and dwindle
  Into the hell from which it first was hurled,
A scoff of impious pride from fiends impure;
      Till human thoughts might kneel alone,
      Each before the judgement-throne
Of its own aweless soul, or of the Power unknown!
  Oh, that the words which make the thoughts obscure
    From which they spring, as clouds of glimmering dew
  From a white lake blot Heaven's blue portraiture,
    Were stripped of their thin masks and various hue

And frowns and smiles and splendours not their own,
   Till in the nakedness of false and true
   They stand before their Lord, each to receive its due!

XVII

He who taught man to vanquish whatsoever
   Can be between the cradle and the grave
Crowned him the King of Life. Oh, vain endeavour!
   If on his own high will, a willing slave,
He has enthroned the oppression and the oppressor.
      What if earth can clothe and feed
      Amplest millions at their need,
And power in thought be as the tree within the seed?
   Or what if Art, an ardent intercessor,
     Driving on fiery wings to Nature's throne,
   Checks the great mother stooping to caress her,
     And cries: 'Give me, thy child, dominion
Over all heights and depth'? if Life can breed
   New wants, and wealth from those who toil and groan,
   Rend of thy gifts and hers a thousandfold for one!

XVIII

Come thou, but lead out of the inmost cave
   Of man's deep spirit, as the morning-star
Beckons the Sun from the Eoan wave,
   Wisdom. I hear the pennons of her car
Self-moving, like cloud charioted by flame;
      Comes she not, and come ye not,
      Rulers of eternal thought,
To judge, with solemn truth, life's ill-apportioned lot?
   Blind Love, and equal Justice, and the Fame
     Of what has been, the Hope of what will be?
   O Liberty! if such could be thy name
     Wert thou disjoined from these, or they from thee:

If thine or theirs were treasures to be bought
By blood or tears, have not the wise and free
Wept tears, and blood like tears? – The solemn harmony

XIX

Paused, and the Spirit of that mighty singing
To its abyss was suddenly withdrawn;
Then, as a wild swan, when sublimely winging
Its path athwart the thunder-smoke of dawn,
Sinks headlong through the aëreal golden light
On the heavy-sounding plain,
When the bolt has pierced its brain;
As summer clouds dissolve, unburthened of their rain;
As a far taper fades with fading night,
As a brief insect dies with dying day, –
My song, its pinions disarrayed of might,
Drooped; o'er it closed the echoes far away
Of the great voice which did its flight sustain,
As waves which lately paved his watery way
Hiss round a drowner's head in their tempestuous play.

TO —

I

I FEAR thy kisses, gentle maiden,
   Thou needest not fear mine;
My spirit is too deeply laden
   Ever to burthen thine.

II

I fear thy mien, thy tones, thy motion,
   Thou needest not fear mine;
Innocent is the heart's devotion
   With which I worship thine.

ARETHUSA

I

ARETHUSA arose
From her couch of snows
In the Acroceraunian mountains, –
  From cloud and from crag,
  With many a jag,
Shepherding her bright fountains.
  She leapt down the rocks,
  With her rainbow locks
Streaming among the streams; –
  Her steps paved with green
  The downward ravine
Which slopes to the western gleams;
  And gliding and springing
  She went, ever singing,
In murmurs as soft as sleep;
  The Earth seemed to love her,
  And Heaven smiled above her,
As she lingered towards the deep.

II

  Then Alpheus bold,
  On his glacier cold,
With his trident the mountains strook;
  And opened a chasm
  In the rocks – with the spasm
All Erymanthus shook.
  And the black south wind
  It unsealed behind
The urns of the silent snow,
  And earthquake and thunder
  Did rend in sunder

The bars of the springs below.
   And the beard and the hair
   Of the River-god were
Seen through the torrent's sweep,
   As he followed the light
   Of the fleet nymph's flight
To the brink of the Dorian deep.

III

   'Oh, save me! Oh, guide me!
   And bid the deep hide me,
For he grasps me now by the hair!'
   The loud Ocean heard,
   To its blue depth stirred,
And divided at her prayer;
   And under the water
   The Earth's white daughter
Fled like a sunny beam;
   Behind her descended
   Her billows, unblended
With the brackish Dorian stream: –
   Like a gloomy stain
   On the emerald main
Alpheus rushed behind, –
   As an eagle pursuing
   A dove to its ruin
Down the streams of the cloudy wind.

IV

   Under the bowers
   Where the Ocean Powers
Sit on their pearlèd thrones;
   Through the coral woods
   Of the weltering floods,
Over heaps of unvalued stones;

Through the dim beams
Which amid the streams
Weave a network of coloured light;
   And under the caves,
   Where the shadowy waves
Are as green as the forest's night: —
   Outspeeding the shark,
   And the sword-fish dark,
Under the Ocean's foam,
   And up through the rifts
   Of the mountain clifts
They passed to their Dorian home.

v

And now from their fountains
In Enna's mountains,
Down one vale where the morning basks,
   Like friends once parted
   Grown single-hearted,
They ply their watery tasks.
   At sunrise they leap
   From their cradles steep
In the cave of the shelving hill;
   At noontide they flow
   Through the woods below
And the meadows of asphodel;
   And at night they sleep
   In the rocking deep
Beneath the Ortygian shore; —
   Like spirits that lie
   In the azure sky
When they love but live no more.

HYMN OF APOLLO

I

THE sleepless Hours who watch me as I lie,
   Curtained with star-inwoven tapestries
From the broad moonlight of the sky,
   Fanning the busy dreams from my dim eyes, –
Waken me when their Mother, the gray Dawn,
Tells them that dreams and that the moon is gone.

II

Then I arise, and climbing Heaven's blue dome,
   I walk over the mountains and the waves,
Leaving my robe upon the ocean foam;
   My footsteps pave the clouds with fire; the caves
Are filled with my bright presence, and the air
Leaves the green Earth to my embraces bare.

III

The sunbeams are my shafts, with which I kill
   Deceit, that loves the night and fears the day;
All men who do or even imagine ill
   Fly me, and from the glory of my ray
Good minds and open actions take new might,
Until diminished by the reign of Night.

IV

I feed the clouds, the rainbows and the flowers
   With their aethereal colours; the moon's globe
And the pure stars in their eternal bowers
   Are cinctured with my power as with a robe;
Whatever lamps on Earth or Heaven may shine
Are portions of one power, which is mine.

V

I stand at noon upon the peak of Heaven,
  Then with unwilling steps I wander down
Into the clouds of the Atlantic even;
  For grief that I depart they weep and frown:
What look is more delightful than the smile
With which I soothe them from the western isle?

VI

I am the eye with which the Universe
  Beholds itself and knows itself divine;
All harmony of instrument or verse,
  All prophecy, all medicine is mine,
All light of art or nature; – to my song
Victory and praise in its own right belong.

HYMN OF PAN

I

FROM the forests and highlands
  We come, we come;
From the river-girt islands,
  Where loud waves are dumb
    Listening to my sweet pipings.
The wind in the reeds and the rushes,
  The bees on the bells of thyme,
The birds on the myrtle bushes,
  The cicale above in the lime,
And the lizards below in the grass,
Were as silent as ever old Tmolus was,
    Listening to my sweet pipings.

II

Liquid Peneus was flowing,
  And all dark Tempe lay
In Pelion's shadow, outgrowing
  The light of the dying day,
    Speeded by my sweet pipings.
The Sileni, and Sylvans, and Fauns,
  And the Nymphs of the woods and the waves
To the edge of the moist river-lawns,
  And the brink of the dewy caves,
And all that did then attend and follow,
Were silent with love, as you now, Apollo,
  With envy of my sweet pipings.

III

I sang of the dancing stars,
  I sang of the daedal Earth,
And of Heaven – and the giant wars,
  And Love, and Death, and Birth, –
    And then I changed my pipings, –
Singing how down the vale of Maenalus
  I pursued a maiden and clasped a reed.
Gods and men, we are all deluded thus!
  It breaks in our bosom and then we bleed:
All wept, as I think both ye now would,
If envy or age had not frozen your blood,
    At the sorrow of my sweet pipings.

THE QUESTION

I

I DREAMED that, as I wandered by the way,
  Bare Winter suddenly was changed to Spring,
And gentle odours led my steps astray,
  Mixed with a sound of waters murmuring
Along a shelving bank of turf, which lay
  Under a copse, and hardly dared to fling
Its green arms round the bosom of the stream,
But kissed it and then fled, as thou mightest in dream.

II

There grew pied wind-flowers and violets,
  Daisies, those pearled Arcturi of the earth,
The constellated flower that never sets;
  Faint oxlips; tender bluebells, at whose birth
The sod scarce heaved; and that tall flower that wets –
  Like a child, half in tenderness and mirth –
Its mother's face with Heaven's collected tears,
When the low wind, its playmate's voice, it hears.

III

And in the warm hedge grew lush eglantine,
  Green cowbind and the moonlight-coloured may,
And cherry-blossoms, and white cups, whose wine
  Was the bright dew, yet drained not by the day;
And wild roses, and ivy serpentine,
  With its dark buds and leaves, wandering astray;
And flowers azure, black, and streaked with gold,
Fairer than any wakened eyes behold.

IV

And nearer to the river's trembling edge
  There grew broad flag-flowers, purple pranked with
    white,
And starry river buds among the sedge,
  And floating water-lilies, broad and bright,
Which lit the oak that overhung the hedge
  With moonlight beams of their own watery light;
And bulrushes, and reeds of such deep green
As soothed the dazzled eye with sober sheen.

V

Methought that of these visionary flowers
  I made a nosegay, bound in such a way
That the same hues, which in their natural bowers
  Were mingled or opposed, the like array
Kept these imprisoned children of the Hours
  Within my hand, – and then, elate and gay,
I hastened to the spot whence I had come,
That I might there present it! – Oh! to whom?

ODE TO NAPLES

EPODE I a

I stood within the City disinterred;
   And heard the autumnal leaves like light footfalls
Of spirits passing through the streets; and heard
The Mountain's slumberous voice at intervals
   Thrill through those roofless halls;
The oracular thunder penetrating shook
  The listening soul in my suspended blood;
I felt that Earth out of her deep heart spoke –
  I felt, but heard not: – through white columns glowed
   The isle-sustaining ocean-flood,
A plane of light between two heavens of azure!
  Around me gleamed many a bright sepulchre
Of whose pure beauty, Time, as if his pleasure
Were to spare Death, had never made erasure;
  But every living lineament was clear
  As in the sculptor's thought; and there
The wreaths of stony myrtle, ivy, and pine,
  Like winter leaves o'ergrown by moulded snow,
  Seemed only not to move and grow
Because the crystal silence of the air
  Weighed on their life; even as the Power divine
  Which then lulled all things, brooded upon mine.

EPODE II a

   Then gentle winds arose
   With many a mingled close
Of wild Aeolian sound, and mountain-odours keen;
   And where the Baian ocean
   Welters with airlike motion,
Within, above, around its bowers of starry green,

Moving the sea-flowers in those purple caves,
 Even as the ever stormless atmosphere
  Floats o'er the Elysian realm,
It bore me, like an Angel, o'er the waves
 Of sunlight, whose swift pinnace of dewy air
  No storm can overwhelm.
  I sailed, where ever flows
  Under the calm Serene
  A spirit of deep emotion
  From the unknown graves
  Of the dead Kings of Melody.
Shadowy Aornos darkened o'er the helm
The horizontal aether; Heaven stripped bare
Its depth over Elysium, where the prow
Made the invisible water white as snow;
From that Typhaean mount, Inarime,
 There streamed a sunbright vapour, like the standard
  Of some aethereal host;
  Whilst from all the coast,
 Louder and louder, gathering round, there wandered
Over the oracular woods and divine sea
Prophesyings which grew articulate –
They seize me – I must speak them! – be they fate!

STROPHE I

Naples! thou Heart of men which ever pantest
 Naked, beneath the lidless eye of Heaven!
Elysian City, which to calm enchantest
 The mutinous air and sea! they round thee, even
 As sleep round Love, are driven!
Metropolis of a ruined Paradise
 Long lost, late won, and yet but half regained!
Bright Altar of the bloodless sacrifice,
 Which armèd Victory offers up unstained
  To Love, the flower-enchained!

Thou which wert once, and then didst cease to be,
Now art, and henceforth ever shalt be, free,
    If Hope, and Truth, and Justice can avail, –
        Hail, hail, all hail!

STROPHE II

    Thou youngest giant birth
    Which from the groaning earth
Leap'st, clothed in armour of impenetrable scale!
    Last of the Intercessors!
    Who 'gainst the Crowned Transgressors
Pleadest before God's love! Arrayed in Wisdom's mail,
    Wave thy lightning lance in mirth
    Nor let thy high heart fail,
Though from their hundred gates the leagued Oppressors
    With hurried legions move!
        Hail, hail, all hail!

ANTISTROPHE I α

What though Cimmerian Anarchs dare blaspheme
    Freedom and thee? thy shield is as a mirror
To make their blind slaves see, and with fierce gleam
    To turn his hungry sword upon the wearer;
        A new Actaeon's error
Shall theirs have been – devoured by their own hounds!
    Be thou like the imperial Basilisk
Killing thy foe with unapparent wounds!
    Gaze on Oppression, till at that dread risk
    Aghast she pass from the Earth's disk:
Fear not, but gaze – for freemen mightier grow,
And slaves more feeble, gazing on their foe: –
    If Hope, and Truth, and Justice may avail,
        Thou shalt be great – All hail!

ANTISTROPHE II α

From Freedom's form divine
From Nature's inmost shrine,
Strip every impious gawd, rend Error veil by veil;
O'er Ruin desolate,
O'er Falsehood's fallen state,
Sit thou sublime, unawed; be the Destroyer pale!
And equal laws be thine,
And wingèd words let sail,
Freighted with truth even from the throne of God:
That wealth, surviving fate,
Be thine. – All hail!

ANTISTROPHE I β

Didst thou not start to hear Spain's thrilling paean
From land to land re-echoed solemnly,
Till silence became music? From the Aeaean
To the cold Alps, eternal Italy
Starts to hear thine! The Sea
Which paves the desert streets of Venice laughs
In light and music; widowed Genoa wan
By moonlight spells ancestral epitaphs,
Murmuring, 'Where is Doria?' fair Milan,
Within whose veins long ran
The viper's palsying venom, lifts her heel
To bruise his head. The signal and the seal
(If Hope and Truth and Justice can avail)
Art thou of all these hopes. – O hail!

ANTISTROPHE II β

Florence! beneath the sun,
Of cities fairest one,
Blushes within her bower for Freedom's expectation:
From eyes of quenchless hope
Rome tears the priestly cope,

As ruling once by power, so now by admiration, –
    An athlete stripped to run
    From a remoter station
For the high prize lost on Philippi's shore: –
    As then Hope, Truth, and Justice did avail,
    So now may Fraud and Wrong! O hail!

EPODE I β

Hear ye the march as of the Earth-born Forms
    Arrayed against the ever-living Gods?
The crash and darkness of a thousand storms
    Bursting their inaccessible abodes
        Of crags and thunder-clouds?
See ye the banners blazoned to the day,
    Inwrought with emblems of barbaric pride?
Dissonant threats kill Silence far away,
    The serene Heaven which wraps our Eden wide
        With iron light is dyed;
The Anarchs of the North lead forth their legions
    Like Chaos o'er creation, uncreating;
An hundred tribes nourished on strange religions
And lawless slaveries, – down the aëreal regions
        Of the white Alps, desolating,
        Famished wolves that bide no waiting,
Blotting the glowing footsteps of old glory,
Trampling our columned cities into dust,
        Their dull and savage lust
        On Beauty's corse to sickness satiating –
They come! The fields they tread look black and hoary
With fire – from their red feet the streams run gory!

EPODE II β

    Great Spirit, deepest Love!
    Which rulest and dost move

All things which live and are, within the Italian shore;
    Who spreadest Heaven around it,
    Whose woods, rocks, waves, surround it;
Who sittest in thy star, o'er Ocean's western floor;
Spirit of Beauty! at whose soft command
  The sunbeams and the showers distil its foison
    From the Earth's bosom chill;
Oh, bid those beams be each a blinding brand
  Of lightning! bid those showers be dews of poison!
    Bid the Earth's plenty kill!
    Bid thy bright Heaven above,
    Whilst light and darkness bound it,
    Be their tomb who planned
    To make it ours and thine!
  Or, with thine harmonizing ardours fill
And raise thy sons, as o'er the prone horizon
Thy lamp feeds every twilight wave with fire –
Be man's high hope and unextinct desire
The instrument to work thy will divine!
  Then clouds from sunbeams, antelopes from leopards,
    And frowns and fears from thee,
    Would not more swiftly flee
  Than Celtic wolves from the Ausonian shepherds. –
Whatever, Spirit, from thy starry shrine
  Thou yieldest or withholdest, oh, let be
  This city of thy worship ever free!

AUTUMN: A DIRGE

I

THE warm sun is failing, the bleak wind is wailing,
The bare boughs are sighing, the pale flowers are dying,
And the Year
On the earth her death-bed, in a shroud of leaves dead,
Is lying.
Come, Months, come away,
From November to May,
In your saddest array;
Follow the bier
Of the dead cold Year,
And like dim shadows watch by her sepulchre.

II

The chill rain is falling, the nipped worm is crawling,
The rivers are swelling, the thunder is knelling
For the Year;
The blithe swallows are flown, and the lizards each gone
To his dwelling;
Come, Months, come away;
Put on white, black, and gray;
Let your light sisters play —
Ye, follow the bier
Of the dead cold Year,
And make her grave green with tear on tear.

TO THE MOON

I

ART thou pale for weariness
Of climbing heaven and gazing on the earth,
   Wandering companionless
Among the stars that have a different birth, –
And ever changing, like a joyless eye
That finds no object worth its constancy?

II

   Thou chosen sister of the Spirit,
That gazes on thee till in thee it pities . . .

EPIPSYCHIDION

Sweet Spirit! Sister of that orphan one,
Whose empire is the name thou weepest on,
In my heart's temple I suspend to thee
These votive wreaths of withered memory.

Poor captive bird! who, from thy narrow cage,
Pourest such music, that it might assuage
The ruggèd hearts of those who prisoned thee,
Were they not deaf to all sweet melody;
This song shall be thy rose: its petals pale
Are dead, indeed, my adopted Nightingale!
But soft and fragrant is the faded blossom,
And it has no thorn left to wound thy bosom.

High, spirit-wingèd Heart! who dost for ever
Beat thine unfeeling bars with vain endeavour,
Till those bright plumes of thought, in which arrayed
It over-soared this low and worldly shade,
Lie shattered; and thy panting, wounded breast
Stains with dear blood its unmaternal nest!
I weep vain tears: blood would less bitter be,
Yet poured forth gladlier, could it profit thee.

Seraph of Heaven! too gentle to be human,
Veiling beneath that radiant form of Woman
All that is insupportable in thee
Of light, and love, and immortality!
Sweet Benediction in the eternal Curse!
Veiled Glory of this lampless Universe!
Thou Moon beyond the clouds! Thou living Form
Among the Dead! Thou Star above the Storm!

Thou Wonder, and thou Beauty, and thou Terror!
Thou Harmony of Nature's art! Thou Mirror
In whom, as in the splendour of the Sun,
All shapes look glorious which thou gazest on!
Ay, even the dim words which obscure thee now
Flash, lightning-like, with unaccustomed glow;
I pray thee that thou blot from this sad song
All of its much mortality and wrong,
With those clear drops, which start like sacred dew
From the twin lights thy sweet soul darkens through,
Weeping, till sorrow becomes ecstasy:
Then smile on it, so that it may not die.

I never thought before my death to see
Youth's vision thus made perfect. Emily,
I love thee; though the world by no thin name
Will hide that love from its unvalued shame.
Would we two had been twins of the same mother!
Or, that the name my heart lent to another
Could be a sister's bond for her and thee,
Blending two beams of one eternity!
Yet were one lawful and the other true,
These names, though dear, could paint not, as is due,
How beyond refuge I am thine. Ah me!
I am not thine: I am a part of *thee*.

Sweet Lamp! my moth-like Muse has burned its wings
Or, like a dying swan who soars and sings,
Young Love should teach Time, in his own gray style,
All that thou art. Art thou not void of guile,
A lovely soul formed to be blessed and bless?
A well of sealed and secret happiness,
Whose waters like blithe light and music are,
Vanquishing dissonance and gloom? A Star

Which moves not in the moving heavens, alone?
A Smile amid dark frowns? a gentle tone
Amid rude voices? a belovèd light?
A Solitude, a Refuge, a Delight?
A Lute, which those whom Love has taught to play
Make music on, to soothe the roughest day
And lull fond Grief asleep? a buried treasure?
A cradle of young thoughts of wingless pleasure?
A violet-shrouded grave of Woe? – I measure
The world of fancies, seeking one like thee,
And find – alas! mine own infirmity.

She met me, Stranger, upon life's rough way,
And lured me towards sweet Death; as Night by Day,
Winter by Spring, or Sorrow by swift Hope,
Led into light, life, peace. An antelope,
In the suspended impulse of its lightness,
Were less aethereally light: the brightness
Of her divinest presence trembles through
Her limbs, as underneath a cloud of dew
Embodied in the windless heaven of June
Amid the splendour-wingèd stars, the Moon
Burns, inextinguishably beautiful:
And from her lips, as from a hyacinth full
Of honey-dew, a liquid murmur drops,
Killing the sense with passion; sweet as stops
Of planetary music heard in trance.
In her mild lights the starry spirits dance,
The sunbeams of those wells which ever leap
Under the lightnings of the soul – too deep
For the brief fathom-line of thought or sense.
The glory of her being, issuing thence,
Stains the dead, blank, cold air with a warm shade
Of unentangled intermixture, made

By Love, of light and motion: one intense
Diffusion, one serene Omnipresence,
Whose flowing outlines mingle in their flowing,
Around her cheeks and utmost fingers glowing
With the unintermitted blood, which there
Quivers, (as in a fleece of snow-like air
The crimson pulse of living morning quiver,)
Continuously prolonged, and ending never,
Till they are lost, and in that Beauty furled
Which penetrates and clasps and fills the world;
Scarce visible from extreme loveliness.
Warm fragrance seems to fall from her light
    dress
And her loose hair; and where some heavy tress
The air of her own speed has disentwined,
The sweetness seems to satiate the faint wind;
And in the soul a wild odour is felt,
Beyond the sense, like fiery dews that melt
Into the bosom of a frozen bud. –
See where she stands! a mortal shape indued
With love and life and light and deity,
And motion which may change but cannot die;
An image of some bright Eternity;
A shadow of some golden dream; a Splendour
Leaving the third sphere pilotless; a tender
Reflection of the eternal Moon of Love
Under whose motions life's dull billows move;
A Metaphor of Spring and Youth and Morning;
A Vision like incarnate April, warning,
With smiles and tears, Frost the Anatomy
Into his summer grave.

                  Ah, woe is me!
What have I dared? where am I lifted? how
Shall I descend, and perish not? I know

That Love makes all things equal: I have heard
By mine own heart this joyous truth averred:
The spirit of the worm beneath the sod
In love and worship, blends itself with God.

   Spouse! Sister! Angel! Pilot of the Fate
Whose course has been so starless! O too late
Belovèd! O too soon adored, by me!
For in the fields of Immortality
My spirit should at first have worshipped thine,
A divine presence in a place divine;
Or should have moved beside it on this earth,
A shadow of that substance, from its birth;
But not as now: — I love thee; yes, I feel
That on the fountain of my heart a seal
Is set, to keep its waters pure and bright
For thee, since in those *tears* thou hast delight.
We — are we not formed, as notes of music are,
For one another, though dissimilar;
Such difference without discord, as can make
Those sweetest sounds, in which all spirits shake
As trembling leaves in a continuous air?

   Thy wisdom speaks in me, and bids me dare
Beacon the rocks on which high hearts are wrecked.
I never was attached to that great sect,
Whose doctrine is, that each one should select
Out of the crowd a mistress or a friend,
And all the rest, though fair and wise, commend
To cold oblivion, though it is in the code
Of modern morals, and the beaten road
Which those poor slaves with weary footsteps
   tread,
Who travel to their home among the dead
By the broad highway of the world, and so

With one chained friend, perhaps a jealous foe,
The dreariest and the longest journey go.

True Love in this differs from gold and clay,
That to divide is not to take away.
Love is like understanding, that grows bright,
Gazing on many truths; 'tis like thy light,
Imagination! which from earth and sky,
And from the depths of human fantasy,
As from a thousand prisms and mirrors, fills
The Universe with glorious beams, and kills
Error, the worm, with many a sun-like arrow
Of its reverberated lightning. Narrow
The heart that loves, the brain that contemplates,
The life that wears, the spirit that creates
One object, and one form, and builds thereby
A sepulchre for its eternity.

Mind from its object differs most in this:
Evil from good; misery from happiness;
The baser from the nobler; the impure
And frail, from what is clear and must endure.
If you divide suffering and dross, you may
Diminish till it is consumed away;
If you divide pleasure and love and thought,
Each part exceeds the whole; and we know not
How much, while any yet remains unshared,
Of pleasure may be gained, of sorrow spared:
This truth is that deep well, whence sages draw
The unenvied light of hope; the eternal law
By which those live, to whom this world of life
Is as a garden ravaged, and whose strife
Tills for the promise of a later birth
The wilderness of this Elysian earth.

There was a Being whom my spirit oft
Met on its visioned wanderings, far aloft,
In the clear golden prime of my youth's dawn,
Upon the fairy isles of sunny lawn,
Amid the enchanted mountains, and the caves
Of divine sleep, and on the air-like waves
Of wonder-level dream, whose tremulous floor
Paved her light steps; – on an imagined shore,
Under the gray beak of some promontory
She met me, robed in such exceeding glory,
That I beheld her not. In solitudes
Her voice came to me through the whispering woods,
And from the fountains, and the odours deep
Of flowers, which, like lips murmuring in their
    sleep
Of the sweet kisses which had lulled them there,
Breathed but of *her* to the enamoured air;
And from the breezes whether low or loud,
And from the rain of every passing cloud,
And from the singing of the summer-birds,
And from all sounds, all silence. In the words
Of antique verse and high romance, – in form
Sound, colour – in whatever checks that Storm
Which with the shattered present chokes the past;
And in that best philosophy, whose taste
Makes this cold common hell, our life, a doom
As glorious as a fiery martyrdom;
Her Spirit was the harmony of truth. –

Then, from the caverns of my dreamy youth
I sprang, as one sandalled with plumes of fire,
And towards the lodestar of my one desire,
I flitted, like a dizzy moth, whose flight
Is as a dead leaf's in the owlet light,

When it would seek in Hesper's setting sphere
A radiant death, a fiery sepulchre,
As if it were a lamp of earthly flame. –
But She, whom prayers or tears then could not tame,
Passed, like a God throned on a wingèd planet,
Whose burning plumes to tenfold swiftness fan it,
Into the dreary cone of our life's shade;
And as a man with mighty loss dismayed,
I would have followed, though the grave between
Yawned like a gulf whose spectres are unseen:
When a voice said: – 'O thou of hearts the weakest,
The phantom is beside thee whom thou seekest.'
Then I – 'Where?' – the world's echo answered 'where?'
And in that silence, and in my despair,
I questioned every tongueless wind that flew
Over my tower of mourning, if it knew
Whither 'twas fled, this soul out of my soul;
And murmured names and spells which have control
Over the sightless tyrants of our fate;
But neither prayer nor verse could dissipate
The night which closed on her; nor uncreate
That world within this Chaos, mine and me,
Of which she was the veiled Divinity,
The world I say of thoughts that worshipped her:
And therefore I went forth, with hope and fear
And every gentle passion sick to death,
Feeding my course with expectation's breath,
Into the wintry forest of our life;
And struggling through its error with vain strife,
And stumbling in my weakness and my haste,
And half bewildered by new forms, I passed,
Seeking among those untaught foresters
If I could find one form resembling hers,
In which she might have masked herself from me.

There, – One, whose voice was venomed melody
Sate by a well, under blue nightshade bowers;
The breath of her false mouth was like faint flowers,
Her touch was as electric poison, – flame
Out of her looks into my vitals came,
And from her living cheeks and bosom flew
A killing air, which pierced like honey-dew
Into the core of my green heart, and lay
Upon its leaves; until, as hair grown gray
O'er a young brow, they hid its unblown prime
With ruins of unseasonable time.

In many mortal forms I rashly sought
The shadow of that idol of my thought.
And some were fair – but beauty dies away:
Others were wise – but honeyed words betray:
And One was true – oh! why not true to me?
Then, as a hunted deer that could not flee,
I turned upon my thoughts, and stood at bay,
Wounded and weak and panting; the cold day
Trembled, for pity of my strife and pain.
When, like a noonday dawn, there shone again
Deliverance. One stood on my path who seemed
As like the glorious shape which I had dreamed
As is the Moon, whose changes ever run
Into themselves, to the eternal Sun;
The cold chaste Moon, the Queen of Heaven's bright isles,
Who makes all beautiful on which she smiles,
That wandering shrine of soft yet icy flame
Which ever is transformed, yet still the same,
And warms not but illumines. Young and fair
As the descended Spirit of that sphere,
She hid me, as the Moon may hide the night
From its own darkness, until all was bright

Between the Heaven and Earth of my calm mind,
And, as a cloud charioted by the wind,
She led me to a cave in that wild place,
And sate beside me, with her downward face
Illumining my slumbers, like the Moon
Waxing and waning o'er Endymion.
And I was laid asleep, spirit and limb,
And all my being became bright or dim
As the Moon's image in a summer sea,
According as she smiled or frowned on me;
And there I lay, within a chaste cold bed:
Alas, I then was nor alive nor dead: —
For at her silver voice came Death and Life,
Unmindful each of their accustomed strife,
Masked like twin babes, a sister and a brother,
The wandering hopes of one abandoned mother,
And through the cavern without wings they flew,
And cried 'Away, he is not of our crew.'
I wept, and though it be a dream, I weep.

What storms then shook the ocean of my sleep,
Blotting that Moon, whose pale and waning lips
Then shrank as in the sickness of eclipse; —
And how my soul was as a lampless sea,
And who was then its Tempest; and when She,
The Planet of that hour, was quenched, what frost
Crept o'er those waters, till from coast to coast
The moving billows of my being fell
Into a death of ice, immovable; —
And then — what earthquakes made it gape and split,
The white Moon smiling all the while on it,
These words conceal: — If not, each word would be
The key of staunchless tears. Weep not for me!

At length, into the obscure Forest came
The Vision I had sought through grief and shame.
Athwart that wintry wilderness of thorns
Flashed from her motion splendour like the Morn's,
And from her presence life was radiated
Through the gray earth and branches bare and dead;
So that her way was paved, and roofed above
With flowers as soft as thoughts of budding love;
And music from her respiration spread
Like light, – all other sounds were penetrated
By the small, still, sweet spirit of that sound,
So that the savage winds hung mute around;
And odours warm and fresh fell from her hair
Dissolving the dull cold in the frore air:
Soft as an Incarnation of the Sun,
When light is changed to love, this glorious One
Floated into the cavern where I lay,
And called my Spirit, and the dreaming clay
Was lifted by the thing that dreamed below
As smoke by fire, and in her beauty's glow
I stood, and felt the dawn of my long night
Was penetrating me with living light:
I knew it was the Vision veiled from me
So many years – that it was Emily.

Twin Spheres of light who rule this passive Earth,
This world of love, this *me*; and into birth
Awaken all its fruits and flowers, and dart
Magnetic might into its central heart;
And lift its billows and its mists, and guide
By everlasting laws, each wind and tide
To its fit cloud, and its appointed cave;
And lull its storms, each in the craggy grave

Which was its cradle, luring to faint bowers
The armies of the rainbow-wingèd showers;
And, as those married lights, which from the towers
Of Heaven look forth and fold the wandering globe
In liquid sleep and splendour, as a robe;
And all their many-mingled influence blend,
If equal, yet unlike, to one sweet end; –
So ye, bright regents, with alternate sway
Govern my sphere of being, night and day!
Thou, not disdaining even a borrowed might;
Thou, not eclipsing a remoter light;
And, through the shadow of the seasons three,
From Spring to Autumn's sere maturity,
Light it into the Winter of the tomb,
Where it may ripen to a brighter bloom.
Thou too, O Comet beautiful and fierce,
Who drew the heart of this frail Universe
Towards thine own; till, wrecked in that convulsion,
Alternating attraction and repulsion,
Thine went astray and that was rent in twain;
Oh, float into our azure heaven again!
Be there Love's folding-star at thy return;
The living Sun will feed thee from its urn
Of golden fire; the Moon will veil her horn
In thy last smiles; adoring Even and Morn
Will worship thee with incense of calm breath
And lights and shadows; as the star of Death
And Birth is worshipped by those sisters wild
Called Hope and Fear – upon the heart are piled
Their offerings, – of this sacrifice divine
A World shall be the altar.

                                   Lady mine,
Scorn not these flowers of thought, the fading birth
Which from its heart of hearts that plant puts forth

Whose fruit, made perfect by thy sunny eyes,
Will be as of the trees of Paradise.

The day is come, and thou wilt fly with me.
To whatso'er of dull mortality
Is mine, remain a vestal sister still;
To the intense, the deep, the imperishable,
Not mine but me, henceforth be thou united
Even as a bride, delighting and delighted.
The hour is come: — the destined Star has risen
Which shall descend upon a vacant prison.
The walls are high, the gates are strong, thick set
The sentinels — but true Love never yet
Was thus constrained: it overleaps all fence:
Like lightning, with invisible violence
Piercing its continents; like Heaven's free breath,
Which he who grasps can hold not; liker Death,
Who rides upon a thought, and makes his way
Through temple, tower, and palace, and the array
Of arms: more strength has Love than he or they;
For it can burst his charnel, and make free
The limbs in chains, the heart in agony,
The soul in dust and chaos.
                              Emily,
A ship is floating in the harbour now,
A wind is hovering o'er the mountain's brow;
There is a path on the sea's azure floor,
No keel has ever ploughed that path before;
The halcyons brood around the foamless isles;
The treacherous Ocean has forsworn its wiles;
The merry mariners are bold and free:
Say, my heart's sister, wilt thou sail with me?
Our bark is as an albatross, whose nest
Is a far Eden of the purple East;

And we between her wings will sit, while Night,
And Day, and Storm, and Calm, pursue their flight,
Our ministers, along the boundless Sea,
Treading each other's heels, unheededly.
It is an isle under Ionian skies,
Beautiful as a wreck of Paradise,
And, for the harbours are not safe and good,
This land would have remained a solitude
But for some pastoral people native there,
Who from the Elysian, clear, and golden air
Draw the last spirit of the age of gold,
Simple and spirited; innocent and bold.
The blue Aegean girds this chosen home,
With ever-changing sound and light and foam,
Kissing the sifted sands, and caverns hoar;
And all the winds wandering along the shore
Undulate with the undulating tide:
There are thick woods where sylvan forms abide;
And many a fountain, rivulet, and pond,
As clear as elemental diamond,
Or serene morning air; and far beyond,
The mossy tracks made by the goats and deer
(Which the rough shepherd treads but once a
    year)
Pierce into glades, caverns, and bowers, and halls
Built round with ivy, which the waterfalls
Illumining, with sound that never fails
Accompany the noonday nightingales;
And all the place is peopled with sweet airs;
The light clear element which the isle wears
Is heavy with the scent of lemon-flowers,
Which floats like mist laden with unseen showers,
And falls upon the eyelids like faint sleep;
And from the moss violets and jonquils peep,

And dart their arrowy odour through the brain
Till you might faint with that delicious pain.
And every motion, odour, beam, and tone,
With that deep music is in unison:
Which is a soul within the soul – they seem
Like echoes of an antenatal dream. –
It is an isle 'twixt Heaven, Air, Earth, and Sea,
Cradled, and hung in clear tranquillity;
Bright as that wandering Eden Lucifer,
Washed by the soft blue Oceans of young air.
It is a favoured place. Famine or Blight,
Pestilence, War and Earthquake, never light
Upon its mountain-peaks; blind vultures, they
Sail onward far upon their fatal way:
The wingèd storms, chanting their thunder-psalm
To other lands, leave azure chasms of calm
Over this isle, or weep themselves in dew,
From which its fields and woods ever renew
Their green and golden immortality.
And from the sea there rise, and from the sky
There fall, clear exhalations, soft and bright,
Veil after veil, each hiding some delight,
Which Sun or Moon or zephyr draw aside,
Till the isle's beauty, like a naked bride
Glowing at once with love and loveliness,
Blushes and trembles at its own excess:
Yet, like a buried lamp, a Soul no less
Burns in the heart of this delicious isle,
An atom of th' Eternal, whose own smile
Unfolds itself, and may be felt, not seen
O'er the gray rocks, blue waves, and forests
    green,
Filling their bare and void interstices. –
But the chief marvel of the wilderness

Is a lone dwelling, built by whom or how
None of the rustic island-people know:
'Tis not a tower of strength, though with its height
It overtops the woods; but, for delight,
Some wise and tender Ocean-King, ere crime
Had been invented, in the world's young prime,
Reared it, a wonder of that simple time,
An envy of the isles, a pleasure-house
Made sacred to his sister and his spouse.
It scarce seems now a wreck of human art,
But, as it were Titanic; in the heart
Of Earth having assumed its form, then grown
Out of the mountains, from the living stone,
Lifting itself in caverns light and high:
For all the antique and learnèd imagery
Has been erased, and in the place of it
The ivy and the wild-vine interknit
The volumes of their many-twining stems;
Parasite flowers illume with dewy gems
The lampless halls, and when they fade, the sky
Peeps through their winter-woof of tracery
With moonlight patches, or star atoms keen,
Or fragments of the day's intense serene; –
Working mosaic on their Parian floors.
And, day and night, aloof, from the high towers
And terraces, the Earth and Ocean seem
To sleep in one another's arms, and dream
Of waves, flowers, clouds, woods, rocks, and all that we
Read in their smiles, and call reality.

  This isle and house are mine, and I have vowed
Thee to be lady of the solitude. –
And I have fitted up some chambers there
Looking towards the golden Eastern air,

And level with the living winds, which flow
Like waves above the living waves below. –
I have sent books and music there, and all
Those instruments with which high Spirits call
The future from its cradle, and the past
Out of its grave, and make the present last
In thoughts and joys which sleep, but cannot die,
Folded within their own eternity.
Our simple life wants little, and true taste
Hires not the pale drudge Luxury, to waste
The scene it would adorn, and therefore still,
Nature with all her children haunts the hill.
The ring-dove, in the embowering ivy, yet
Keeps up her love-lament, and the owls flit
Round the evening tower, and the young stars glance
Between the quick bats in their twilight dance;
The spotted deer bask in the fresh moonlight
Before our gate, and the slow, silent night
Is measured by the pants of their calm sleep.
Be this our home in life, and when years heap
Their withered hours, like leaves, on our decay,
Let us become the overhanging day,
The living soul of this Elysian isle,
Conscious, inseparable, one. Meanwhile
We two will rise, and sit, and walk together,
Under the roof of blue Ionian weather,
And wander in the meadows, or ascend
The mossy mountains, where the blue heavens bend
With lightest winds, to touch their paramour;
Or linger, where the pebble-paven shore,
Under the quick, faint kisses of the sea
Trembles and sparkles as with ecstasy, –
Possessing and possessed by all that is
Within that calm circumference of bliss,

And by each other, till to love and live
Be one: – or, at the noontide hour, arrive
Where some old cavern hoar seems yet to keep
The moonlight of the expired night asleep,
Through which the awakened day can never peep;
A veil for our seclusion, close as night's,
Where secure sleep may kill thine innocent lights;
Sleep, the fresh dew of languid love, the rain
Whose drops quench kisses till they burn again.
And we will talk, until thought's melody
Become too sweet for utterance, and it die
In words, to live again in looks, which dart
With thrilling tone into the voiceless heart,
Harmonizing silence without a sound.
Our breath shall intermix, our bosoms bound,
And our veins beat together; and our lips
With other eloquence than words, eclipse
The soul that burns between them, and the wells
Which boil under our being's inmost cells,
The fountains of our deepest life, shall be
Confused in Passion's golden purity,
As mountain-springs under the morning sun.
We shall become the same, we shall be one
Spirit within two frames, oh! wherefore two?
One passion in twin-hearts, which grows and
    grew,
Till like two meteors of expanding flame,
Those spheres instinct with it become the same,
Touch, mingle, are transfigured; ever still
Burning, yet ever inconsumable:
In one another's substance finding food,
Like flames too pure and light and unimbued
To nourish their bright lives with baser prey,
Which point to Heaven and cannot pass away:

One hope within two wills, one will beneath
Two overshadowing minds, one life, one death,
One Heaven, one Hell, one immortality,
And one annihilation. Woe is me!
The wingèd words on which my soul would pierce
Into the height of Love's rare Universe,
Are chains of lead around its flight of fire –
I pant, I sink, I tremble, I expire!

   Weak Verses, go, kneel at your Sovereign's feet,
And say: – 'We are the masters of thy slave;
What wouldest thou with us and ours and thine?'
Then call your sisters from Oblivion's cave,
All singing loud: 'Love's very pain is sweet,
But its reward is in the world divine
Which, if not here, it builds beyond the grave.'
So shall ye live when I am there. Then haste
Over the hearts of men, until ye meet
Marina, Vanna, Primus, and the rest,
And bid them love each other and be blessed:
And leave the troop which errs, and which reproves,
And come and be my guest, – for I am Love's.

TO NIGHT

I

Swiftly walk o'er the western wave,
    Spirit of Night!
Out of the misty eastern cave,
Where, all the long and lone daylight,
Thou wovest dreams of joy and fear,
Which make thee terrible and dear, –
    Swift be thy flight!

II

Wrap thy form in a mantle gray,
    Star-inwrought!
Blind with thine hair the eyes of Day;
Kiss her until she be wearied out,
Then wander o'er city, and sea, and land,
Touching all with thine opiate wand –
    Come, long-sought!

III

When I arose and saw the dawn,
    I sighed for thee;
When light rode high, and the dew was gone,
And noon lay heavy on flower and tree,
And the weary Day turned to his rest,
Lingering like an unloved guest,
    I sighed for thee.

IV

Thy brother Death came, and cried,
    Wouldst thou me?
Thy sweet child Sleep, the filmy-eyed,

Murmured like a noontide bee,
Shall I nestle near thy side?
Wouldst thou me? – And I replied,
  No, not thee!

V

Death will come when thou art dead,
  Soon, too soon –
Sleep will come when thou art fled;
Of neither would I ask the boon
I ask of thee, belovèd Night –
Swift be thine approaching flight,
  Come soon, soon!

TIME

UNFATHOMABLE Sea! whose waves are years,
  Ocean of Time, whose waters of deep woe
Are brackish with the salt of human tears!
  Thou shoreless flood, which in thy ebb and flow
Claspest the limits of mortality,
And sick of prey, yet howling on for more,
Vomitest thy wrecks on its inhospitable shore;
  Treacherous in calm, and terrible in storm,
    Who shall put forth on thee,
    Unfathomable Sea!

FROM THE ARABIC: AN IMITATION

I

My faint spirit was sitting in the light
    Of thy looks, my love;
It panted for thee like the hind at noon
    For the brooks, my love.
Thy barb whose hoofs outspeed the tempest's flight
    Bore thee far from me;
My heart, for my weak feet were weary soon,
    Did companion thee.

II

Ah! fleeter far than fleetest storm or steed,
    Or the death they bear,
The heart which tender thought clothes like a dove
    With the wings of care;
In the battle, in the darkness, in the need,
    Shall mine cling to thee,
Nor claim one smile for all the comfort, love,
    It may bring to thee.

TO EMILIA VIVIANI

I

MADONNA, wherefore hast thou sent to me
  Sweet-basil and mignonette?
Embleming love and health, which never yet
In the same wreath might be.
  Alas, and they are wet!
Is it with thy kisses or thy tears?
    For never rain or dew
    Such fragrance drew
From plant or flower – the very doubt endears
    My sadness ever new,
The sighs I breathe, the tears I shed for thee.

II

Send the stars light, but send not love to me,
  In whom love ever made
Health like a heap of embers soon to fade –

MUSIC, when soft voices die,
Vibrates in the memory —
Odours, when sweet violets sicken,
Live within the sense they quicken.

Rose leaves, when the rose is dead,
Are heaped for the belovèd's bed;
And so thy thoughts, when thou art gone,
Love itself shall slumber on.

ADONAIS

I

I WEEP for Adonais – he is dead!
O, weep for Adonais! though our tears
Thaw not the frost which binds so dear a head!
And thou, sad Hour, selected from all years
To mourn our loss, rouse thy obscure compeers,
And teach them thine own sorrow, say: 'With me
Died Adonais; till the Future dares
Forget the Past, his fate and fame shall be
An echo and a light unto eternity!'

II

Where wert thou, mighty Mother, when he lay,
When thy Son lay, pierced by the shaft which flies
In darkness? where was lorn Urania
When Adonais died? With veilèd eyes,
'Mid listening Echoes, in her Paradise
She sate, while one, with soft enamoured breath,
Rekindled all the fading melodies,
With which, like flowers that mock the corse beneath,
He had adorned and hid the coming bulk of Death.

III

Oh, weep for Adonais – he is dead!
Wake, melancholy Mother, wake and weep!
Yet wherefore? Quench within their burning bed
Thy fiery tears, and let thy loud heart keep
Like his, a mute and uncomplaining sleep;
For he is gone, where all things wise and fair
Descend; – oh, dream not that the amorous Deep
Will yet restore him to the vital air;
Death feeds on his mute voice, and laughs at our despair.

IV

Most musical of mourners, weep again!
Lament anew, Urania! – He died,
Who was the Sire of an immortal strain,
Blind, old, and lonely, when his country's pride,
The priest, the slave, and the liberticide,
Trampled and mocked with many a loathèd rite
Of lust and blood; he went, unterrified,
Into the gulf of death; but his clear Sprite
Yet reigns o'er earth; the third among the sons of light.

V

Most musical of mourners, weep anew!
Not all to that bright station dared to climb;
And happier they their happiness who knew,
Whose tapers yet burn through that night of time
In which suns perished; others more sublime,
Struck by the envious wrath of man or god,
Have sunk, extinct in their refulgent prime;
And some yet live, treading the thorny road,
Which leads, through toil and hate, to Fame's serene
    abode.

VI

But now, thy youngest, dearest one, has perished –
The nursling of thy widowhood, who grew,
Like a pale flower by some sad maiden cherished,
And fed with true-love tears, instead of dew;
Most musical of mourners, weep anew!
Thy extreme hope, the loveliest and the last,
The bloom, whose petals nipped before they blew
Died on the promise of the fruit, is waste;
The broken lily lies – the storm is overpast.

VII

To that high Capital, where kingly Death
Keeps his pale court in beauty and decay,
He came; and bought, with price of purest breath,
A grave among the eternal. – Come away!
Haste, while the vault of blue Italian day
Is yet his fitting charnel-roof! while still
He lies, as if in dewy sleep he lay;
Awake him not! surely he takes his fill
Of deep and liquid rest, forgetful of all ill.

VIII

He will awake no more, oh, never more! –
Within the twilight chamber spreads apace
The shadow of white Death, and at the door
Invisible Corruption waits to trace
His extreme way to her dim dwelling-place;
The eternal Hunger sits, but pity and awe
Soothe her pale rage, nor dares she to deface
So fair a prey, till darkness, and the law
Of change, shall o'er his sleep the mortal curtain draw.

IX

Oh, weep for Adonais! – The quick Dreams,
The passion-wingèd Ministers of thought,
Who were his flocks, whom near the living streams
Of his young spirit he fed, and whom he taught
The love which was its music, wander not, –
Wander no more, from kindling brain to brain,
But droop there, whence they sprung; and mourn their
 lot
Round the cold heart, where, after their sweet pain,
They ne'er will gather strength, or find a home again.

X

And one with trembling hands clasps his cold head,
And fans him with her moonlight wings, and cries;
'Our love, our hope, our sorrow, is not dead;
See, on the silken fringe of his faint eyes,
Like dew upon a sleeping flower, there lies
A tear some Dream has loosened from his brain.'
Lost Angel of a ruined Paradise!
She knew not 'twas her own; as with no stain
She faded, like a cloud which had outwept its rain.

XI

One from a lucid urn of starry dew
Washed his light limbs as if embalming them;
Another clipped her profuse locks, and threw
The wreath upon him, like an anadem,
Which frozen tears instead of pearls begem;
Another in her wilful grief would break
Her bow and wingèd reeds, as if to stem
A greater loss with one which was more weak;
And dull the barbèd fire against his frozen cheek.

XII

Another Splendour on his mouth alit,
That mouth, whence it was wont to draw the breath
Which gave it strength to pierce the guarded wit,
And pass into the panting heart beneath
With lightning and with music: the damp death
Quenched its caress upon his icy lips;
And, as a dying meteor stains a wreath
Of moonlight vapour, which the cold night clips,
It flushed through his pale limbs, and passed to its eclipse.

XIII

And others came . . . Desires and Adorations,
Wingèd Persuasions and veiled Destinies,
Splendours, and Glooms, and glimmering Incarnations
Of hopes and fears, and twilight Phantasies;
And Sorrow, with her family of Sighs,
And Pleasure, blind with tears, led by the gleam
Of her own dying smile instead of eyes,
Came in slow pomp; – the moving pomp might seem
Like pageantry of mist on an autumnal stream.

XIV

All he had loved, and moulded into thought,
From shape, and hue, and odour, and sweet sound,
Lamented Adonais. Morning sought
Her eastern watch-tower, and her hair unbound,
Wet with the tears which should adorn the ground,
Dimmed the aëreal eyes that kindle day;
Afar the melancholy thunder moaned,
Pale Ocean in unquiet slumber lay,
And the wild Winds flew round, sobbing in their dismay.

XV

Lost Echo sits amid the voiceless mountains,
And feeds her grief with his remembered lay,
And will no more reply to winds or fountains,
Or amorous birds perched on the young green spray,
Or herdsman's horn, or bell at closing day;
Since she can mimic not his lips, more dear
Than those for whose disdain she pined away
Into a shadow of all sounds: – a drear
Murmur, between their songs, is all the woodmen hear.

XVI

Grief made the young Spring wild, and she threw down
Her kindling buds, as if she Autumn were,
Or they dead leaves; since her delight is flown,
For whom should she have waked the sullen year?
To Phoebus was not Hyacinth so dear
Nor to himself Narcissus, as to both
Thou, Adonais: wan they stand and sere
Amid the faint companions of their youth,
With dew all turned to tears; odour, to sighing ruth.

XVII

Thy spirit's sister, the lorn nightingale
Mourns not her mate with such melodious pain;
Not so the eagle, who like thee could scale
Heaven, and could nourish in the sun's domain
Her mighty youth with morning, doth complain,
Soaring and screaming round her empty nest,
As Albion wails for thee: the curse of Cain
Light on his head who pierced thy innocent breast,
And scared the angel soul that was its earthly guest!

XVIII

Ah, woe is me! Winter is come and gone,
But grief returns with the revolving year;
The airs and streams renew their joyous tone;
The ants, the bees, the swallows reappear;
Fresh leaves and flowers deck the dead Season's bier;
The amorous birds now pair in every brake,
And build their mossy homes in field and brere;
And the green lizard, and the golden snake,
Like unimprisoned flames, out of their trance awake.

XIX

Through wood and stream and field and hill and Ocean
A quickening life from the Earth's heart has burst
As it has ever done, with change and motion,
From the great morning of the world when first
God dawned on Chaos; in its stream immersed,
The lamps of Heaven flash with a softer light;
All baser things pant with life's sacred thirst;
Diffuse themselves; and spend in love's delight,
The beauty and the joy of their renewèd might.

XX

The leprous corpse, touched by this spirit tender,
Exhales itself in flowers of gentle breath;
Like incarnations of the stars, when splendour
Is changed to fragrance, they illumine death
And mock the merry worm that wakes beneath;
Nought we know, dies. Shall that alone which knows
Be as a sword consumed before the sheath
By sightless lightning? – the intense atom glows
A moment, then is quenched in a most cold repose.

XXI

Alas! that all we loved of him should be,
But for our grief, as if it had not been,
And grief itself be mortal! Woe is me!
Whence are we, and why are we? of what scene
The actors or spectators? Great and mean
Meet massed in death, who lends what life must borrow.
As long as skies are blue, and fields are green,
Evening must usher night, night urge the morrow,
Month follow month with woe, and year wake year to
    sorrow.

XXII

He will awake no more, oh, never more!
'Wake thou,' cried Misery, 'childless Mother, rise
Out of thy sleep, and slake, in thy heart's core,
A wound more fierce than his, with tears and sighs.'
And all the Dreams that watched Urania's eyes,
And all the Echoes whom their sister's song
Had held in holy silence, cried: 'Arise!'
Swift as a Thought by the snake Memory stung,
From her ambrosial rest the fading Splendour sprung.

XXIII

She rose like an autumnal Night, that springs
Out of the East, and follows wild and drear
The golden Day, which, on eternal wings,
Even as a ghost abandoning a bier,
Had left the Earth a corpse. Sorrow and fear
So struck, so roused, so rapt Urania;
So saddened round her like an atmosphere
Of stormy mist; so swept her on her way
Even to the mournful place where Adonais lay.

XXIV

Out of her secret Paradise she sped,
Through camps and cities rough with stone, and steel,
And human hearts, which to her aery tread
Yielding not, wounded the invisible
Palms of her tender feet where'er they fell:
And barbèd tongues, and thoughts more sharp than they,
Rent the soft Form they never could repel,
Whose scared blood, like the young tears of May,
Paved with eternal flowers that undeserving way.

XXV

In the death-chamber for a moment Death,
Shamed by the presence of that living Might,
Blushed to annihilation, and the breath
Revisited those lips, and Life's pale light
Flashed through those limbs, so late her dear delight.
'Leave me not wild and drear and comfortless,
As silent lightning leaves the starless night!
Leave me not!' cried Urania: her distress
Roused Death: Death rose and smiled, and met her vain
    caress.

XXVI

'Stay yet awhile! speak to me once again;
Kiss me, so long but as a kiss may live;
And in my heartless breast and burning brain
That word, that kiss, shall all thoughts else survive,
With food of saddest memory kept alive,
Now thou art dead, as if it were a part
Of thee, my Adonais! I would give
All that I am to be as thou now art!
But I am chained to Time, and cannot thence depart!

XXVII

'O gentle child, beautiful as thou wert,
Why didst thou leave the trodden paths of men
Too soon, and with weak hands though mighty heart
Dare the unpastured dragon in his den?
Defenceless as thou wert, oh, where was then
Wisdom the mirrored shield, or scorn the spear?
Or hadst thou waited the full cycle, when
Thy spirit should have filled its crescent sphere,
The monsters of life's waste had fled from thee like deer.

XXVIII

'The herded wolves, bold only to pursue;
The obscene ravens, clamorous o'er the dead;
The vultures to the conqueror's banner true
Who feed where Desolation first has fed,
And whose wings rain contagion; – how they fled,
When, like Apollo, from his golden bow
The Pythian of the age one arrow sped
And smiled! – The spoilers tempt no second blow,
They fawn on the proud feet that spurn them lying low.

XXIX

'The sun comes forth, and many reptiles spawn;
He sets, and each ephemeral insect then
Is gathered into death without a dawn,
And the immortal stars awake again;
So is it in the world of living men:
A godlike mind soars forth, in its delight
Making earth bare and veiling heaven, and when
It sinks, the swarms that dimmed or shared its light
Leave to its kindred lamps the spirit's awful night.'

XXX

Thus ceased she: and the mountain shepherds came,
Their garlands sere, their magic mantles rent;
The Pilgrim of Eternity, whose fame
Over his living head like Heaven is bent,
An early but enduring monument,
Came, veiling all the lightnings of his song
In sorrow; from her wilds Ierne sent
The sweetest lyrist of her saddest wrong,
And Love taught Grief to fall like music from his tongue.

XXXI

Midst others of less note, came one frail Form,
A phantom among men; companionless
As the last cloud of an expiring storm
Whose thunder is its knell; he, as I guess,
Had gazed on Nature's naked loveliness,
Actaeon-like, and now he fled astray
With feeble steps o'er the world's wilderness,
And his own thoughts, along that rugged way,
Pursued, like raging hounds, their father and their prey.

XXXII

A pardlike Spirit beautiful and swift –
A Love in desolation masked; – a Power
Girt round with weakness; – it can scarce uplift
The weight of the superincumbent hour;
It is a dying lamp, a falling shower,
A breaking billow; – even whilst we speak
Is it not broken? On the withering flower
The killing sun smiles brightly: on a cheek
The life can burn in blood, even while the heart may break.

XXXIII

His head was bound with pansies overblown,
And faded violets, white, and pied, and blue;
And a light spear topped with a cypress cone,
Round whose rude shaft dark ivy-tresses grew
Yet dripping with the forest's noonday dew,
Vibrated, as the ever-beating heart
Shook the weak hand that grasped it; of that crew
He came the last, neglected and apart;
A herd-abandoned deer struck by the hunter's dart.

XXXIV

All stood aloof, and at his partial moan
Smiled through their tears; well knew that gentle band
Who in another's fate now wept his own,
As in the accents of an unknown land
He sung new sorrow; sad Urania scanned
The Stranger's mien, and murmured: 'Who art thou?'
He answered not, but with a sudden hand
Made bare his branded and ensanguined brow,
Which was like Cain's or Christ's – oh! that it should be so!

XXXV

What softer voice is hushed over the dead?
Athwart what brow is that dark mantle thrown?
What form leans sadly o'er the white death-bed,
In mockery of monumental stone,
The heavy heart heaving without a moan?
If it be He, who, gentlest of the wise,
Taught, soothed, loved, honoured the departed one,
Let me not vex, with inharmonious sighs,
The silence of that heart's accepted sacrifice.

XXXVI

Our Adonais has drunk poison – oh!
What deaf and viperous murderer could crown
Life's early cup with such a draught of woe?
The nameless worm would now itself disown:
It felt, yet could escape, the magic tone
Whose prelude held all envy, hate, and wrong,
But what was howling in one breast alone,
Silent with expectation of the song,
Whose master's hand is cold, whose silver lyre unstrung.

XXXVII

Live thou, whose infamy is not thy fame!
Live! fear no heavier chastisement from me,
Thou noteless blot on a remembered name!
But be thyself, and know thyself to be!
And ever at thy season be thou free
To spill the venom when thy fangs o'erflow;
Remorse and Self-contempt shall cling to thee;
Hot Shame shall burn upon thy secret brow,
And like a beaten hound tremble thou shalt – as now.

XXXVIII

Nor let us weep that our delight is fled
Far from these carrion kites that scream below;
He wakes or sleeps with the enduring dead;
Thou canst not soar where he is sitting now. –
Dust to the dust! but the pure spirit shall flow
Back to the burning fountain whence it came,
A portion of the Eternal, which must glow
Through time and change, unquenchably the same,
Whilst thy cold embers choke the sordid hearth of shame.

XXXIX

Peace, peace! he is not dead, he doth not sleep –
He hath awakened from the dream of life –
'Tis we, who lost in stormy visions, keep
With phantoms an unprofitable strife,
And in mad trance, strike with our spirit's knife
Invulnerable nothings. – *We* decay
Like corpses in a charnel; fear and grief
Convulse us and consume us day by day,
And cold hopes swarm like worms within our living clay.

XL

He has outsoared the shadow of our night;
Envy and calumny and hate and pain,
And that unrest which men miscall delight,
Can touch him not and torture not again;
From the contagion of the world's slow stain
He is secure, and now can never mourn
A heart grown cold, a head grown gray in vain;
Nor, when the spirit's self has ceased to burn,
With sparkless ashes load an unlamented urn.

XLI

He lives, he wakes – 'tis Death is dead, not he;
Mourn not for Adonais. – Thou young Dawn,
Turn all thy dew to splendour, for from thee
The spirit thou lamentest is not gone;
Ye caverns and ye forests, cease to moan!
Cease, ye faint flowers and fountains, and thou Air,
Which like a mourning veil thy scarf hadst thrown
O'er the abandoned Earth, now leave it bare
Even to the joyous stars which smile on its despair!

XLII

He is made one with Nature: there is heard
His voice in all her music, from the moan
Of thunder, to the song of night's sweet bird;
He is a presence to be felt and known
In darkness and in light, from herb and stone,
Spreading itself where'er that Power may move
Which has withdrawn his being to its own;
Which wields the world with never-wearied love,
Sustains it from beneath, and kindles it above.

XLIII

He is a portion of the loveliness
Which once he made more lovely: he doth bear
His part, while the one Spirit's plastic stress
Sweeps through the dull dense world, compelling there,
All new successions to the forms they wear;
Torturing th' unwilling dross that checks its flight
To its own likeness, as each mass may bear;
And bursting in its beauty and its might
From trees and beasts and men into the Heaven's light.

XLIV

The splendours of the firmament of time
May be eclipsed, but are extinguished not,
Like stars to their appointed height they climb,
And death is a low mist which cannot blot
The brightness it may veil. When lofty thought
Lifts a young heart above its mortal lair,
And love and life contend in it, for what
Shall be its earthly doom, the dead live there
And move like winds of light on dark and stormy air.

XLV

The inheritors of unfulfilled renown
Rose from their thrones, built beyond mortal thought,
Far in the Unapparent. Chatterton
Rose pale, – his solemn agony had not
Yet faded from him; Sidney, as he fought
And as he fell and as he lived and loved
Sublimely mild, a Spirit without spot,
Arose; and Lucan, by his death approved:
Oblivion as they rose shrank like a thing reproved.

XLVI

And many more, whose names on Earth are dark,
But whose transmitted effluence cannot die
So long as fire outlives the parent spark,
Rose, robed in dazzling immortality.
'Thou art become as one of us,' they cry,
'It was for thee yon kingless sphere has long
Swung blind in unascended majesty,
Silent alone amid an Heaven of Song.
Assume thy wingèd throne, thou Vesper of our throng!'

XLVII

Who mourns for Adonais? Oh, come forth,
Fond wretch! and know thyself and him aright.
Clasp with thy panting soul the pendulous Earth;
As from a centre, dart thy spirit's light
Beyond all worlds, until its spacious might
Satiate the void circumference: then shrink
Even to a point within our day and night;
And keep thy heart light lest it make thee sink
When hope has kindled hope, and lured thee to the brink.

XLVIII

Or go to Rome, which is the sepulchre,
Oh, not of him, but of our joy: 'tis nought
That ages, empires, and religions there
Lie buried in the ravage they have wrought;
For such as he can lend, – they borrow not
Glory from those who made the world their prey;
And he is gathered to the kings of thought
Who waged contention with their time's decay,
And of the past are all that cannot pass away.

XLIX

Go thou to Rome, – at once the Paradise,
The grave, the city, and the wilderness;
And where its wrecks like shattered mountains rise,
And flowering weeds, and fragrant copses dress
The bones of Desolation's nakedness
Pass, till the spirit of the spot shall lead
Thy footsteps to a slope of green access
Where, like an infant's smile, over the dead
A light of laughing flowers along the grass is spread;

L

And gray walls moulder round, on which dull Time
Feeds, like slow fire upon a hoary brand;
And one keen pyramid with wedge sublime,
Pavilioning the dust of him who planned
This refuge for his memory, doth stand
Like flame transformed to marble; and beneath,
A field is spread, on which a newer band
Have pitched in Heaven's smile their camp of death,
Welcoming him we lose with scarce extinguished breath.

LI

Here pause: these graves are all too young as yet
To have outgrown the sorrow which consigned
Its charge to each; and if the seal is set,
Here, on one fountain of a mourning mind,
Break it not thou! too surely shalt thou find
Thine own well full, if thou returnest home,
Of tears and gall. From the world's bitter wind
Seek shelter in the shadow of the tomb.
What Adonais is, why fear we to become?

LII

The One remains, the many change and pass;
Heaven's light forever shines, Earth's shadows fly;
Life, like a dome of many-coloured glass,
Stains the white radiance of Eternity,
Until Death tramples it to fragments. – Die,
If thou wouldst be with that which thou dost seek!
Follow where all is fled! – Rome's azure sky,
Flowers, ruins, statues, music, words, are weak
The glory they transfuse with fitting truth to speak.

LIII

Why linger, why turn back, why shrink, my Heart?
Thy hopes are gone before: from all things here
They have departed; thou shouldst now depart!
A light is passed from the revolving year,
And man, and woman; and what still is dear
Attracts to crush, repels to make thee wither.
The soft sky smiles, – the low wind whispers near:
'Tis Adonais calls! oh, hasten thither,
No more let Life divide what Death can join together.

LIV

That Light whose smile kindles the Universe,
That Beauty in which all things work and move,
That Benediction which the eclipsing Curse
Of birth can quench not, that sustaining Love
Which through the web of being blindly wove
By man and beast and earth and air and sea,
Burns bright or dim, as each are mirrors of
The fire for which all thirst; now beams on me,
Consuming the last clouds of cold mortality.

LV

The breath whose might I have invoked in song
Descends on me; my spirit's bark is driven,
Far from the shore, far from the trembling throng
Whose sails were never to the tempest given;
The massy earth and spherèd skies are riven!
I am borne darkly, fearfully, afar;
Whilst, burning through the inmost veil of Heaven,
The soul of Adonais, like a star,
Beacons from the abode where the Eternal are.

HELLAS

I

WORLDS on worlds are rolling ever
　　From creation to decay,
Like the bubbles on a river
　　Sparkling, bursting, borne away.
　　But they are still immortal
　　Who, through birth's orient portal
And death's dark chasm hurrying to and fro,
　　Clothe their unceasing flight
　　In the brief dust and light
Gathered around their chariots as they go;
　　New shapes they still may weave,
　　New gods, new laws receive,
Bright or dim are they as the robes they last
　　On Death's bare ribs had cast.

A power from the unknown God,
　　A Promethean conqueror, came;
Like a triumphal path he trod
　　The thorns of death and shame.
　　A mortal shape to him
　　Was like the vapour dim
Which the orient planet animates with light;
　　Hell, Sin, and Slavery came,
　　Like bloodhounds mild and tame,
Nor preyed, until their Lord had taken flight;
　　The moon of Mahomet
　　Arose, and it shall set:
While blazoned as on Heaven's immortal noon
　　The cross leads generations on.

Swift as the radiant shapes of sleep
  From one whose dreams are Paradise
Fly, when the fond wretch wakes to weep,
  And Day peers forth with her blank eyes;
  So fleet, so faint, so fair,
  The Powers of earth and air
Fled from the folding-star of Bethlehem:
  Apollo, Pan, and Love,
  And even Olympian Jove
Grew weak, for killing Truth had glared on them;
  Our hills and seas and streams,
  Dispeopled of their dreams,
Their waters turned to blood, their dew to tears,
  Wailed for the golden years.

II

The world's great age begins anew,
  The golden years return,
The earth doth like a snake renew
  Her winter weeds outworn:
Heaven smiles, and faiths and empires gleam,
Like wrecks of a dissolving dream.

A brighter Hellas rears its mountains
  From waves serener far;
A new Peneus rolls his fountains
  Against the morning star.
Where fairer Tempes bloom, there sleep
Young Cyclads on a sunnier deep.

A loftier Argo cleaves the main,
  Fraught with a later prize;
Another Orpheus sings again,
  And loves, and weeps, and dies.

A new Ulysses leaves once more
Calypso for his native shore.

Oh, write no more the tale of Troy,
   If earth Death's scroll must be!
Nor mix with Laian rage the joy
   Which dawns upon the free:
Although a subtler Sphinx renew
Riddles of death Thebes never knew.

Another Athens shall arise,
   And to remoter time
Bequeath, like sunset to the skies,
   The splendour of its prime;
And leave, if nought so bright may live,
All earth can take or Heaven can give.

Saturn and Love their long repose
   Shall burst, more bright and good
Than all who fell, than One who rose,
   Than many unsubdued:
Not gold, not blood, their altar dowers,
But votive tears and symbol flowers.

Oh, cease! must hate and death return?
   Cease! must men kill and die?
Cease! drain not to its dregs the urn
   Of bitter prophecy.
The world is weary of the past,
Oh, might it die or rest at last!

SONG

I

RARELY, rarely, comest thou,
  Spirit of Delight!
Wherefore hast thou left me now
  Many a day and night?
Many a weary night and day
'Tis since thou art fled away.

II

How shall ever one like me
  Win thee back again?
With the joyous and the free
  Thou wilt scoff at pain.
Spirit false! thou hast forgot
  All but those who need thee not.

III

As a lizard with the shade
  Of a trembling leaf,
Thou with sorrow art dismayed;
  Even the sighs of grief
Reproach thee, that thou art not near,
And reproach thou wilt not hear.

IV

Let me set my mournful ditty
  To a merry measure;
Thou wilt never come for pity,
  Thou wilt come for pleasure;
Pity then will cut away
Those cruel wings, and thou wilt stay.

V

I love all that thou lovest,
   Spirit of Delight!
The fresh Earth in new leaves dressed,
   And the starry night;
Autumn evening, and the morn
When the golden mists are born.

VI

I love snow, and all the forms
   Of the radiant frost;
I love waves, and winds, and storms,
   Everything almost
Which is Nature's, and may be
Untainted by man's misery.

VII

I love tranquil solitude
   And such society
As is quiet, wise, and good;
   Between thee and me
What difference? but thou dost possess
The things I seek, not love them less.

VIII

I love Love – though he has wings,
   And like light can flee,
But above all other things,
   Spirit, I love thee –
Thou art love and life! Oh, come,
Make once more my heart thy home.

A LAMENT

I

O world! O life! O time!
On whose last steps I climb,
   Trembling at that where I had stood before;
When will return the glory of your prime?
            No more – Oh, never more!

II

Out of the day and night
A joy has taken flight;
   Fresh spring, and summer, and winter hoar,
Move my faint heart with grief, but with delight
            No more – Oh, never more!

REMEMBRANCE

I

Swifter far than summer's flight –
Swifter far than youth's delight –
Swifter far than happy night,
 Art thou come and gone –
As the earth when leaves are dead,
As the night when sleep is sped,
As the heart when joy is fled,
 I am left lone, alone.

II

The swallow summer comes again –
The owlet night resumes her reign –
But the wild-swan youth is fain
 To fly with thee, false as thou. –
My heart each day desires the morrow;
Sleep itself is turned to sorrow;
Vainly would my winter borrow
 Sunny leaves from any bough.

III

Lilies for a bridal bed –
Roses for a matron's head –
Violets for a maiden dead –
 Pansies let *my* flowers be:
On the living grave I bear
Scatter them without a tear –
Let no friend, however dear,
 Waste one hope, one fear for me.

TO EDWARD WILLIAMS

I

THE serpent is shut out from Paradise.
  The wounded deer must seek the herb no more
    In which its heart-cure lies:
  The widowed dove must cease to haunt a bower
Like that from which its mate with feignèd sighs
    Fled in the April hour.
  I too must seldom seek again
Near happy friends a mitigated pain.

II

Of hatred I am proud, – with scorn content;
  Indifference, that once hurt me, now is grown
    Itself indifferent;
  But, not to speak of love, pity alone
Can break a spirit already more than bent.
    The miserable one
  Turns the mind's poison into food, –
Its medicine is tears, – its evil good.

III

Therefore, if now I see you seldomer,
  Dear friends, dear *friend*! know that I only fly
    Your looks, because they stir
  Griefs that should sleep, and hopes that cannot die:
The very comfort that they minister
    I scarce can bear, yet I,
  So deeply is the arrow gone,
Should quickly perish if it were withdrawn.

IV

When I return to my cold home, you ask
    Why I am not as I have ever been.
      You spoil me for the task
    Of acting a forced part in life's dull scene, –
Of wearing on my brow the idle mask
      Of author, great or mean,
    In the world's carnival. I sought
Peace thus, and but in you I found it not.

V

Full half an hour, to-day, I tried my lot
    With various flowers, and every one still said,
      'She loves me – loves me not.'
    And if this meant a vision long since fled –
If it meant fortune, fame, or peace of thought –
      If it meant, – but I dread
    To speak what you may know too well:
Still there was truth in the sad oracle.

VI

The crane o'er seas and forests seeks her home;
    No bird so wild but has its quiet nest,
      When it no more would roam;
    The sleepless billows on the ocean's breast
Break like a bursting heart, and die in foam,
      And thus at length find rest:
    Doubtless there is a place of peace
Where *my* weak heart and all its throbs will cease.

VII

I asked her, yesterday, if she believed
    That I had resolution. One who *had*
      Would ne'er have thus relieved

His heart with words, – but what his judgement bade
Would do, and leave the scorner unrelieved.
These verses are too sad
To send to you, but that I know,
Happy yourself, you feel another's woe.

TO —

I

ONE word is too often profaned
    For me to profane it,
One feeling too falsely disdained
    For thee to disdain it;
One hope is too like despair
    For prudence to smother,
And pity from thee more dear
    Than that from another.

II

I can give not what men call love,
    But wilt thou accept not
The worship the heart lifts above
    And the Heavens reject not, —
The desire of the moth for the star,
    Of the night for the morrow,
The devotion to something afar
    From the sphere of our sorrow?

TO —

I

WHEN passion's trance is overpast,
If tenderness and truth could last,
Or live, whilst all wild feelings keep
Some mortal slumber, dark and deep,
I should not weep, I should not weep!

II

It were enough to feel, to see,
Thy soft eyes gazing tenderly,
And dream the rest – and burn and be
The secret food of fires unseen,
Couldst thou but be as thou hast been.

III

After the slumber of the year
The woodland violets reappear;
All things revive in field or grove,
And sky and sea, but two, which move
And form all others, life and love.

LINES: 'WHEN THE LAMP IS SHATTERED'

I

When the lamp is shattered
The light in the dust lies dead –
  When the cloud is scattered
The rainbow's glory is shed.
  When the lute is broken,
Sweet tones are remembered not;
  When the lips have spoken,
Loved accents are soon forgot.

II

  As music and splendour
Survive not the lamp and the lute,
  The heart's echoes render
No song when the spirit is mute: –
  No song but sad dirges,
Like the wind through a ruined cell,
  Or the mournful surges
That ring the dead seaman's knell.

III

When hearts have once mingled
Love first leaves the well-built nest;
  The weak one is singled
To endure what it once possessed.
  O Love! who bewailest
The frailty of all things here,
  Why choose you the frailest
For your cradle, your home, and your bier?

IV

Its passions will rock thee
As the storms rock the ravens on high;
    Bright reason will mock thee,
Like the sun from a wintry sky.
    From thy nest every rafter
Will rot, and thine eagle home
    Leave thee naked to laughter,
When leaves fall and cold winds come.

From TRANSLATION OF CALDERON'S
EL MAGICO PRODIGIOSO

JUSTINA

'Tis that enamoured Nightingale
  Who gives me the reply;
He ever tells the same soft tale
  Of passion and of constancy
To his mate, who rapt and fond,
Listening sits, a bough beyond.

Be silent, Nightingale – no more
  Make me think, in hearing thee
Thus tenderly thy love deplore,
  If a bird can feel his so,
  What a man would feel for me.
  And, voluptuous Vine, O thou
Who seekest most when least pursuing, –
  To the trunk thou interlacest
  Art the verdure which embracest,
And the weight which is its ruin, –
No more, with green embraces, Vine,
  Make me think on what thou lovest, –
For while thus thy boughs entwine,
  I fear lest thou shouldst teach me, sophist,
How arms might be entangled too.

Light-enchanted Sunflower, thou
Who gazest ever true and tender
On the sun's revolving splendour!
Follow not his faithless glance
With thy faded countenance,

Nor teach my beating heart to fear,
If leaves can mourn without a tear,
How eyes must weep! O Nightingale,
Cease from thy enamoured tale, –
Leafy Vine, unwreathe thy bower,
  Restless Sunflower, cease to move, –
Or tell me all, what poisonous Power
  Ye use against me –

ALL.

Love! Love! Love!

TO JANE: THE INVITATION

Best and brightest, come away!
Fairer far than this fair Day,
Which, like thee to those in sorrow,
Comes to bid a sweet good-morrow
To the rough Year just awake
In its cradle on the brake.
The brightest hour of unborn Spring,
Through the winter wandering,
Found, it seems, the halcyon Morn
To hoar February born.
Bending from Heaven, in azure mirth,
It kissed the forehead of the Earth,
And smiled upon the silent sea,
And bade the frozen streams be free,
And waked to music all their fountains,
And breathed upon the frozen mountains,
And like a prophetess of May
Strewed flowers upon the barren way,
Making the wintry world appear
Like one on whom thou smilest dear.
Away, away, from men and towns,
To the wild wood and the downs –
To the silent wilderness
Where the soul need not repress
Its music lest it should not find
An echo in another's mind,
While the touch of Nature's art
Harmonizes heart to heart.
I leave this notice on my door
For each accustomed visitor: –
'I am gone into the fields
To take what this sweet hour yields; –

Reflection, you may come to-morrow,
Sit by the fireside with Sorrow. –
You with the unpaid bill, Despair, –
You, tiresome verse-reciter, Care, –
I will pay you in the grave, –
Death will listen to your stave.
Expectation too, be off!
To-day is for itself enough;
Hope, in pity mock not Woe
With smiles, nor follow where I go;
Long having lived on thy sweet food,
At length I find one moment's good
After long pain – with all your love,
This you never told me of.'

Radiant Sister of the Day,
Awake! arise! and come away!
To the wild woods and the plains,
And the pools where winter rains
Image all their roof of leaves,
Where the pine its garland weaves
Of sapless green and ivy dun
Round stems that never kiss the sun;
Where the lawns and pastures be,
And the sandhills of the sea, –
Where the melting hoar-frost wets
The daisy-star that never sets,
And wind-flowers, and violets,
Which yet join not scent to hue,
Crown the pale year weak and new;
When the night is left behind
In the deep east, dun and blind,
And the blue noon is over us,
And the multitudinous

Billows murmur at our feet,
Where the earth and ocean meet,
And all things seem only one
In the universal sun.

TO JANE: THE RECOLLECTION

I

Now the last day of many days,
  All beautiful and bright as thou,
    The loveliest and the last, is dead,
Rise, Memory, and write its praise!
    Up, – to thy wonted work! come, trace
      The epitaph of glory fled, –
For now the Earth has changed its face,
    A frown is on the Heaven's brow.

II

We wandered to the Pine Forest
    That skirts the Ocean's foam,
The lightest wind was in its nest,
    The tempest in its home.
The whispering waves were half asleep,
    The clouds were gone to play,
And on the bosom of the deep
    The smile of Heaven lay;
It seemed as if the hour were one
    Sent from beyond the skies,
Which scattered from above the sun
    A light of Paradise.

III

We paused amid the pines that stood
    The giants of the waste,
Tortured by storms to shapes as rude
    As serpents interlaced,

And soothed by every azure breath,
  That under Heaven is blown,
To harmonies and hues beneath,
  As tender as its own;
Now all the tree-tops lay asleep,
  Like green waves on the sea,
As still as in the silent deep
  The ocean woods may be.

IV

How calm it was! – the silence there
  By such a chain was bound
That even the busy woodpecker
  Made stiller by her sound
The inviolable quietness;
  The breath of peace we drew
With its soft motion made not less
  The calm that round us grew.
There seemed from the remotest seat
  Of the white mountain waste,
To the soft flower beneath our feet,
  A magic circle traced, –
A spirit interfused around,
  A thrilling, silent life, –
To momentary peace it bound
  Our mortal nature's strife;
And still I felt the centre of
  The magic circle there
Was one fair form that filled with love
  The lifeless atmosphere.

V

We paused beside the pools that lie
  Under the forest bough, –
Each seemed as 'twere a little sky

291

Gulfed in a world below;
A firmament of purple light
  Which in the dark earth lay,
More boundless than the depth of night,
  And purer than the day –
In which the lovely forests grew,
  As in the upper air,
More perfect both in shape and hue
  Than any spreading there.
There lay the glade and neighbouring lawn,
  And through the dark green wood
The white sun twinkling like the dawn
  Out of a speckled cloud.
Sweet views which in our world above
  Can never well be seen,
Were imaged by the water's love
  Of that fair forest green.
And all was interfused beneath
  With an Elysian glow,
An atmosphere without a breath,
  A softer day below.
Like one beloved the scene had lent
  To the dark water's breast,
Its every leaf and lineament
  With more than truth expressed;
Until an envious wind crept by,
  Like an unwelcome thought,
Which from the mind's too faithful eye
  Blots one dear image out.
Though thou art ever fair and kind,
  The forests ever green,
Less oft is peace in Shelley's mind,
  Than calm in waters, seen.

WITH A GUITAR, TO JANE

ARIEL to Miranda: – Take
This slave of Music, for the sake
Of him who is the slave of thee
And teach it all the harmony
In which thou canst, and only thou,
Make the delighted spirit glow,
Till joy denies itself again,
And, too intense, is turned to pain;
For by permission and command
Of thine own Prince Ferdinand,
Poor Ariel sends this silent token
Of more than ever can be spoken;
Your guardian spirit, Ariel, who,
From life to life, must still pursue
Your happiness; – for thus alone
Can Ariel ever find his own.
From Prospero's enchanted cell,
As the mighty verses tell,
To the throne of Naples, he
Lit you o'er the trackless sea,
Flitting on, your prow before,
Like a living meteor.
When you die, the silent Moon,
In her interlunar swoon,
Is not sadder in her cell
Than deserted Ariel.
When you live again on earth,
Like an unseen star of birth,
Ariel guides you o'er the sea
Of life from your nativity.

Many changes have been run
Since Ferdinand and you begun
Your course of love, and Ariel still
Has tracked your steps, and served your will;
Now, in humbler, happier lot,
This is all remembered not;
And now, alas! the poor sprite is
Imprisoned, for some fault of his,
In a body like a grave; –
From you he only dares to crave,
For his service and his sorrow,
A smile to-day, a song to-morrow.
The artist who this idol wrought,
To echo all harmonious thought,
Felled a tree, while on the steep
The woods were in their winter sleep,
Rocked in that repose divine
On the wind-swept Apennine;
And dreaming, some of Autumn past,
And some of Spring approaching fast,
And some of April buds and showers,
And some of songs in July bowers,
And all of love; and so this tree, –
O that such our death may be! –
Died in sleep, and felt no pain,
To live in happier form again:
From which, beneath Heaven's fairest star,
The artist wrought this loved Guitar,
And taught it justly to reply,
To all who question skilfully,
In language gentle as thine own;
Whispering in enamoured tone
Sweet oracles of woods and dells,
And summer winds in sylvan cells;

For it had learned all harmonies
Of the plains and of the skies,
Of the forests and the mountains,
And the many-voicèd fountains;
The clearest echoes of the hills,
The softest notes of falling rills,
The melodies of birds and bees,
The murmuring of summer seas,
And pattering rain, and breathing dew,
And airs of evening; and it knew
That seldom-heard mysterious sound,
Which, driven on its diurnal round,
As it floats through boundless day,
Our world enkindles on its way. –
All this it knows, but will not tell
To those who cannot question well
The Spirit that inhabits it;
It talks according to the wit
Of its companions; and no more
Is heard than has been felt before,
By those who tempt it to betray
These secrets of an elder day:
But, sweetly as its answers will
Flatter hands of perfect skill,
It keeps its highest, holiest tone
For our belovèd Jane alone.

TO JANE: 'THE KEEN STARS
WERE TWINKLING'

I

The keen stars were twinkling,
And the fair moon was rising among them,
    Dear Jane!
  The guitar was tinkling,
But the notes were not sweet till you sung them
    Again.

II

  As the moon's soft splendour
O'er the faint cold starlight of Heaven
    Is thrown,
  So your voice most tender
To the strings without soul had then given
    Its own.

III

  The stars will awaken,
Though the moon sleep a full hour later,
    To-night;
  No leaf will be shaken
Whilst the dews of your melody scatter
    Delight.

IV

  Though the sound overpowers,
Sing again, with your dear voice revealing
    A tone
  Of some world far from ours,
Where music and moonlight and feeling
    Are one.

LINES WRITTEN IN THE BAY
OF LERICI

SHE left me at the silent time
When the moon had ceased to climb
The azure path of Heaven's steep,
And like an albatross asleep,
Balanced on her wings of light,
Hovered in the purple night,
Ere she sought her ocean nest
In the chambers of the West.
She left me, and I stayed alone
Thinking over every tone
Which, though silent to the ear,
The enchanted heart could hear,
Like notes which die when born, but still
Haunt the echoes of the hill;
And feeling ever – oh, too much! –
The soft vibration of her touch
As if her gentle hand, even now,
Lightly trembled on my brow;
And thus, although she absent were,
Memory gave me all of her
That even Fancy dares to claim: –
Her presence had made weak and tame
All passions, and I lived alone
In the time which is our own;
The past and future were forgot,
As they had been, and would be, not.
But soon, the guardian angel gone,
The daemon reassumed his throne
In my faint heart. I dare not speak
My thoughts, but thus disturbed and weak

I sat and saw the vessels glide
Over the ocean bright and wide,
Like spirit-wingèd chariots sent
O'er some serenest element
For ministrations strange and far;
As if to some Elysian star
Sailed for drink to medicine
Such sweet and bitter pain as mine.
And the wind that winged their flight
From the land came fresh and light,
And the scent of wingèd flowers,
And the coolness of the hours
Of dew, and sweet warmth left by day,
Were scattered o'er the twinkling bay.
And the fisher with his lamp
And spear about the low rocks damp
Crept, and struck the fish which came
To worship the delusive flame.
Too happy they, whose pleasure sought
Extinguishes all sense and thought
Of the regret that pleasure leaves,
Destroying life alone, not peace!

CHARLES THE FIRST

'A WIDOW bird sate mourning for her love
   Upon a wintry bough;
The frozen wind crept on above,
   The freezing stream below.

'There was no leaf upon the forest bare,
   No flower upon the ground,
And little motion in the air
   Except the mill-wheel's sound.'

THE TRIUMPH OF LIFE

SWIFT as a spirit hastening to his task
Of glory and of good, the Sun sprang forth
Rejoicing in his splendour, and the mask

Of darkness fell from the awakened Earth –
The smokeless altars of the mountain snows
Flamed above crimson clouds, and at the birth

Of light, the Ocean's orison arose,
To which the birds tempered their matin lay.
All flowers in field or forest which unclose

Their trembling eyelids to the kiss of day,
Swinging their censers in the element
With orient incense lit by the new ray

Burned slow and inconsumably, and sent
Their odorous sighs up to the smiling air;
And, in succession due, did continent,

Isle, ocean, and all things that in them wear
The form and character of mortal mould,
Rise as the Sun their father rose, to bear

Their portion of the toil, which he of old
Took as his own, and then imposed on them:
But I, whom thoughts which must remain untold

Had kept as wakeful as the stars that gem
The cone of night, now they were laid asleep
Stretched my faint limbs beneath the hoary stem

Which an old chestnut flung athwart the steep
Of a green Apennine: before me fled
The night; behind me rose the day; the deep

Was at my feet, and Heaven above my head, –
When a strange trance over my fancy grew
Which was not slumber, for the shade it spread

Was so transparent, that the scene came through
As clear as when a veil of light is drawn
O'er evening hills they glimmer; and I knew

That I had felt the freshness of that dawn
Bathe in the same cold dew my brow and hair,
And sate as thus upon that slope of lawn

Under the self-same bough, and heard as there
The birds, the fountains and the ocean hold
Sweet talk in music through the enamoured air,
And then a vision on my brain was rolled.

—

As in that trance of wondrous thought I lay,
This was the tenour of my waking dream: –
Methought I sate beside a public way

Thick strewn with summer dust, and a great stream
Of people there was hurrying to and fro
Numerous as gnats upon the evening gleam,

All hastening onward, yet none seemed to know
Whither he went, or whence he came, or why
He made one of the multitude, and so

Was borne amid the crowd, as through the sky
One of the million leaves of summer's bier;
Old age and youth, manhood and infancy,

Mixed in one mighty torrent did appear,
Some flying from the thing they feared, and some
Seeking the object of another's fear;

And others, as with steps towards the tomb,
Pored on the trodden worms that crawled beneath,
And others mournfully within the gloom

Of their own shadow walked, and called it death;
And some fled from it as it were a ghost,
Half fainting in the affliction of vain breath:

But more, with motions which each other crossed,
Pursued or shunned the shadows the clouds threw,
Or birds within the noonday aether lost,

Upon that path where flowers never grew, –
And, weary with vain toil and faint for thirst,
Heard not the fountains, whose melodious dew

Out of their mossy cells forever burst;
Nor felt the breeze which from the forest told
Of grassy paths and wood-lawns interspersed

With overarching elms and caverns cold,
And violet banks where sweet dreams brood, but they
Pursued their serious folly as of old.

And as I gazed, methought that in the way
The throng grew wilder, as the woods of June
When the south wind shakes the extinguished day,

And a cold glare, intenser than the noon,
But icy cold, obscured with blinding light
The sun, as he the stars. Like the young moon --

When on the sunlit limits of the night
Her white shell trembles amid crimson air,
And whilst the sleeping tempest gathers might –

Doth, as the herald of its coming, bear
The ghost of its dead mother, whose dim form
Bends in dark aether from her infant's chair, –

So came a chariot on the silent storm
Of its own rushing splendour, and a Shape
So sate within, as one whom years deform,

Beneath a dusky hood and double cape,
Crouching within the shadow of a tomb;
And o'er what seemed the head a cloud-like crape

Was bent, a dun and faint aethereal gloom
Tempering the light. Upon the chariot-beam
A Janus-visaged Shadow did assume

The guidance of that wonder-wingèd team;
The shapes which drew it in thick lightenings
Were lost: – I heard alone on the air's soft stream

The music of their ever-moving wings.
All the four faces of that Charioteer
Had their eyes banded; little profit brings

Speed in the van and blindness in the rear,
Nor then avail the beams that quench the sun, –
Or that with banded eyes could pierce the sphere

Of all that is, has been or will be done;
So ill was the car guided – but it passed
With solemn speed majestically on.

The crowd gave way, and I arose aghast,
Or seemed to rise, so mighty was the trance,
And saw, like clouds upon the thunder-blast,

The million with fierce song and maniac dance
Raging around – such seemed the jubilee
As when to greet some conqueror's advance

Imperial Rome poured forth her living sea
From senate-house, and forum, and theatre,
When   upon the free

Had bound a yoke, which soon they stooped to bear.
Nor wanted here the just similitude
Of a triumphal pageant, for where'er

The chariot rolled, a captive multitude
Was driven; – all those who had grown old in power
Or misery, – all who had their age subdued

By action or by suffering, and whose hour
Was drained to its last sand in weal or woe,
So that the trunk survived both fruit and flower; –

All those whose fame or infamy must grow
Till the great winter lay the form and name
Of this green earth with them for ever low; –

All but the sacred few who could not tame
Their spirits to the conquerors – but as soon
As they had touched the world with living flame,

Fled back like eagles to their native noon,
Or those who put aside the diadem
Of earthly thrones or gems . . .

Were there, of Athens or Jerusalem,
Were neither mid the mighty captives seen,
Nor mid the ribald crowd that followed them,

Nor those who went before fierce and obscene.
The wild dance maddens in the van, and those
Who lead it – fleet as shadows on the green,

Outspeed the chariot, and without repose
Mix with each other in tempestuous measure
To savage music, wilder as it grows,

They, tortured by their agonizing pleasure,
Convulsed and on the rapid whirlwinds spun
Of that fierce Spirit, whose unholy leisure

Was soothed by mischief since the world begun
Throw back their heads and loose their streaming hair;
And in their dance round her who dims the sun,

Maidens and youths fling their wild arms in air
As their feet twinkle; they recede, and now
Bending within each other's atmosphere,

Kindle invisibly – and as they glow
Like moths by light attracted and repelled,
Oft to their bright destruction come and go,

Till like two clouds into one vale impelled,
That shake the mountains when their lightnings mingle
And die in rain – the fiery band which held

Their natures, snaps – while the shock still may tingle:
One falls and then another in the path
Senseless – nor is the desolation single,

Yet ere I can say *where* – the chariot hath
Passed over them – nor other trace I find
But as of foam after the ocean's wrath

Is spent upon the desert shore; – behind,
Old men and women foully disarrayed,
Shake their gray hairs in the insulting wind,

And follow in the dance, with limbs decayed,
Seeking to reach the light which leaves them still
Farther behind and deeper in·the shade.

But not the less with impotence of will
They wheel, though ghastly shadows interpose
Round them and round each other, and fulfil

Their work, and in the dust from whence they rose
Sink, and corruption veils them as they lie,
And past in these performs what   in those.

Struck to the heart by this sad pageantry,
Half to myself I said – 'And what is this?
Whose shape is that within the car? And why –'

I would have added – 'is all here amiss? – '
But a voice answered – 'Life!' – I turned, and knew
(O Heaven, have mercy on such wretchedness!)

That what I thought was an old root which grew
To strange distortion out of the hill side,
Was indeed one of those deluded crew,

And that the grass, which methought hung so wide
And white, was but his thin discoloured hair,
And that the holes he vainly sought to hide,

Were or had been eyes: – 'If thou canst, forbear
To join the dance, which I had well forborne!'
Said the grim Feature (of my thought aware).

'I will unfold that which to this deep scorn
Led me and my companions, and relate
The progress of the pageant since the morn;

'If thirst of knowledge shall not then abate,
Follow it thou even to the night, but I
Am weary.' – Then like one who with the weight

Of his own words is staggered, wearily
He paused; and ere he could resume, I cried:
'First, who art thou?' – 'Before thy memory,

'I feared, loved, hated, suffered, did and died,
And if the spark with which Heaven lit my spirit
Had been with purer nutriment supplied,

'Corruption would not now thus much inherit
Of what was once Rousseau, – nor this disguise
in that which ought to have disdained to wear it;

306

'If I have been extinguished, yet there rise
A thousand beacons from the spark I bore' –
'And who are those chained to the car?' – 'The wise,

'The great, the unforgotten, – they who wore
Mitres and helms and crowns, or wreaths of light,
Signs of thought's empire over thought – their lore

'Taught them not this, to know themselves; their might
Could not repress the mystery within,
And for the morn of truth they feigned, deep night

'Caught them ere evening.' – 'Who is he with chin
Upon his breast, and hands crossed on his chain?' –
'The child of a fierce hour; he sought to win

'The world, and lost all that it did contain
Of greatness, in its hope destroyed; and more
Of fame and peace than virtue's self can gain

'Without the opportunity which bore
Him on its eagle pinions to the peak
From which a thousand climbers have before

'Fallen, as Napoleon fell.' – I felt my cheek
Alter, to see the shadow pass away,
Whose grasp had left the giant world so weak

That every pigmy kicked it as it lay;
And much I grieved to think how power and will
In opposition rule our mortal day,

And why God made irreconcilable
Good and the means of good; and for despair
I half disdained mine eyes' desire to fill

With the spent vision of the times that were
And scarce have ceased to be. – 'Dost thou behold,'
Said my guide, 'those spoilers spoiled, Voltaire,

'Frederick, and Paul, Catherine, and Leopold
And hoary anarchs, demagogues, and sage –
   names which the world thinks always old,

'For in the battle Life and they did wage,
She remained conqueror. I was overcome
By my own heart alone, which neither age,

'Nor tears, nor infamy, nor now the tomb
Could temper to its object.' – 'Let them pass,'
I cried, 'the world and its mysterious doom

'Is not so much more glorious than it was,
That I desire to worship those who drew
New figures on its false and fragile glass

'As the old faded.' – 'Figures ever new
Rise on the bubble, paint them as you may;
We have but thrown, as those before us threw,

'Our shadows on it as it passed away.
But mark how chained to the triumphal chair
The mighty phantoms of an elder day;

'All that is mortal of great Plato there
Expiates the joy and woe his master knew not;
The star that ruled his doom was far too fair,

'And life, where long that flower of Heaven grew not,
Conquered that heart by love, which gold, or pain,
Or age, or sloth, or slavery could subdue not.

'And near him walk the   twain,
The tutor and his pupil, whom Dominion
Followed as tame as vulture in a chain.

'The world was darkened beneath either pinion
Of him whom from the flock of conquerors
Fame singled out for her thunder-bearing minion;

'The other long outlived both woes and wars,
Throned in the thoughts of men, and still had kept
The jealous key of Truth's eternal doors,

'If Bacon's eagle spirit had not lept
Like lightning out of darkness – he compelled
The Proteus shape of Nature, as it slept

'To wake, and lead him to the caves that held
The treasure of the secrets of its reign.
See the great bards of elder time, who quelled

'The passions which they sung, as by their strain
May well be known: their living melody
Tempers its own contagion to the vein

'Of those who are infected with it – I
Have suffered what I wrote, or viler pain!
And so my words have seeds of misery –

'Even as the deeds of others, not as theirs.'
And then he pointed to a company,

'Midst whom I quickly recognized the heirs
Of Caesar's crime, from him to Constantine;
The anarch chiefs, whose force and murderous snares

Had founded many a sceptre-bearing line,
And spread the plague of gold and blood abroad:
And Gregory and John, and men divine,

Who rose like shadows between man and God;
Till that eclipse, still hanging over heaven,
Was worshipped by the world o'er which they strode,

For the true sun it quenched – 'Their power was given
But to destroy,' replied the leader: – 'I
Am one of those who have created, even

'If it be but a world of agony.' –
'Whence camest thou? and whither goest thou?
How did thy course begin?' I said, 'and why?

'Mine eyes are sick of this perpetual flow
Of people, and my heart sick of one sad thought –
Speak!' – 'Whence I am, I partly seem to know,

'And how and by what paths I have been brought
To this dread pass, methinks even thou mayst guess; –
Why this should be, my mind can compass not;

'Whither the conqueror hurries me, still less; –
But follow thou, and from spectator turn
Actor or victim in this wretchedness,

'And what thou wouldst be taught I then may learn
From thee. Now listen: – In the April prime,
When all the forest-tips began to burn

'With kindling green, touched by the azure clime
Of the young season, I was laid asleep
Under a mountain, which from unknown time

'Had yawned into a cavern, high and deep;
And from it came a gentle rivulet,
Whose water, like clear air, in its calm sweep

'Bent the soft grass, and kept for ever wet
The stems of the sweet flowers, and filled the grove
With sounds, which whoso hears must needs forget

'All pleasure and all pain, all hate and love,
Which they had known before that hour of rest;
A sleeping mother then would dream not of

'Her only child who died upon the breast
At eventide – a king would mourn no more
The crown of which his brows were dispossessed

'When the sun lingered o'er his ocean floor
To gild his rival's new prosperity.
Thou wouldst forget thus vainly to deplore

'Ills, which if ills can find no cure from thee,
The thought of which no other sleep will quell,
Nor other music blot from memory,

'So sweet and deep is the oblivious spell;
And whether life had been before that sleep
The Heaven which I imagine, or a Hell

'Like this harsh world in which I wake to weep,
I know not. I arose, and for a space
The scene of woods and waters seemed to keep,

'Though it was now broad day, a gentle trace
Of light diviner than the common sun
Sheds on the common earth, and all the place

'Was filled with magic sounds woven into one
Oblivious melody, confusing sense
Amid the gliding waves and shadows dun;

'And, as I looked, the bright omnipresence
Of morning through the orient cavern flowed,
And the sun's image radiantly intense

'Burned on the waters of the well that glowed
Like gold, and threaded all the forest's maze
With winding paths of emerald fire; there stood

'Amid the sun, as he amid the blaze
Of his own glory, on the vibrating
Floor of the fountain, paved with flashing rays,

'A Shape all light, which with one hand did fling
Dew on the earth, as if she were the dawn,
And the invisible rain did ever sing

'A silver music on the mossy lawn;
And still before me on the dusky grass,
Iris her many-coloured scarf had drawn:

'In her right hand she bore a crystal glass,
Mantling with bright Nepenthe; the fierce splendour
Fell from her as she moved under the mass

'Of the deep cavern, and with palms so tender,
Their tread broke not the mirror of its billow
Glided along the river, and did bend her

'Head under the dark boughs, till like a willow
Her fair hair swept the bosom of the stream
That whispered with delight to be its pillow.

'As one enamoured is upborne in dream
O'er lily-paven lakes, mid silver mist,
To wondrous music, so this shape might seem

'Partly to tread the waves with feet which kissed
The dancing foam; partly to glide along
The air which roughened the moist amethyst,

'Or the faint morning beams that fell among
The trees, or the soft shadows of the trees;
And her feet, ever to the ceaseless song

'Of leaves, and winds, and waves, and birds, and bees,
And falling drops, moved in a measure new
Yet sweet, as on the summer evening breeze,

'Up from the lake a shape of golden dew
Between two rocks, athwart the rising moon,
Dances i' the wind, where never eagle flew;

'And still her feet, no less than the sweet tune
To which they moved, seemed as they moved to blot
The thoughts of him who gazed on them; and soon

'All that was, seemed as if it had been not;
And all the gazer's mind was strewn beneath
Her feet like embers; and she, thought by thought,

'Trampled its sparks into the dust of death;
As day upon the threshold of the east
Treads out the lamps of night, until the breath

'Of darkness re-illumine even the least
Of heaven's living eyes – like day she came
Making the night a dream; and ere she ceased

'To move, as one between desire and shame
Suspended, I said – If, as it doth seem,
Thou comest from the realm without a name

'Into this valley of perpetual dream,
Show whence I came, and where I am, and why –
Pass not away upon the passing stream.

'Arise and quench thy thirst, was her reply.
And as a shut lily stricken by the wand
Of dewy morning's vital alchemy,

'I rose; and, bending at her sweet command,
Touched with faint lips the cup she raised,
And suddenly my brain became as sand

'Where the first wave had more than half erased
The track of deer on desert Labrador;
Whilst the wolf, from which they fled amazed,

'Leaves his stamp visibly upon the shore,
Until the second bursts; – so on my sight
Burst a new vision, never seen before,

'And the fair shape waned in the coming light,
As veil by veil the silent splendour drops
From Lucifer, amid the chrysolite

Of sunrise, ere it tinge the mountain-tops;
And as the presence of that fairest planet,
Although unseen, is felt by one who hopes

'That his day's path may end as he began it,
In that star's smile, whose light is like the scent
Of a jonquil when evening breezes fan it,

'Or the soft note in which his dear lament
The Brescian shepherd breathes, or the caress
That turned his weary slumber to content;

'So knew I in that light's severe excess
The presence of that Shape which on the stream
Moved, as I moved along the wilderness,

'More dimly than a day-appearing dream,
The ghost of a forgotten form of sleep;
A light of heaven, whose half-extinguished beam

'Through the sick day in which we wake to weep
Glimmers, for ever sought, for ever lost;
So did that shape its obscure tenour keep

'Beside my path, as silent as a ghost;
But the new Vision, and the cold bright car,
With solemn speed and stunning music, crossed

'The forest, and as if from some dread war
Triumphantly returning, the loud million
Fiercely extolled the fortune of her star.

'A moving arch of victory, the vermilion
And green and azure plumes of Iris had
Built high over her wind-wingèd pavilion,

'And underneath aethereal glory clad
The wilderness, and far before her flew
The tempest of the splendour, which forbade

'Shadow to fall from leaf and stone; the crew
Seemed in that light, like atomies to dance
Within a sunbeam; – some upon the new

'Embroidery of flowers, that did enhance
The grassy vesture of the desert, played,
Forgetful of the chariot's swift advance;

'Others stood gazing, till within the shade
Of the great mountain its light left them dim;
Others outspeeded it; and others made

'Circles around it, like the clouds that swim
Round the high moon in a bright sea of air;
And more did follow, with exulting hymn,

'The chariot and the captives fettered there: –
But all like bubbles on an eddying flood
Fell into the same track at last, and were

'Borne onward. – I among the multitude
Was swept – me, sweetest flowers delayed not long;
Me, not the shadow nor the solitude;

'Me, not that falling stream's Lethean song;
Me, not the phantom of that early Form
Which moved upon its motion – but among

'The thickest billows of that living storm
I plunged, and bared my bosom to the clime
Of that cold light, whose airs too soon deform.

'Before the chariot had begun to climb
The opposing steep of that mysterious dell,
Behold a wonder worthy of the rhyme

'Of him who from the lowest depths of hell,
Through every paradise and through all glory,
Love led serene, and who returned to tell

'The words of hate and awe; the wondrous story
How all things are transfigured except Love;
For deaf as is a sea, which wrath makes hoary,

'The world can hear not the sweet notes that move
The sphere whose light is melody to lovers –
A wonder worthy of his rhyme. – The grove

'Grew dense with shadows to its inmost covers,
The earth was gray with phantoms, and the air
Was peopled with dim forms, as when there hovers

'A flock of vampire-bats before the glare
Of the tropic sun, bringing, ere evening,
Strange night upon some Indian isle; – thus were

'Phantoms diffused around; and some did fling
Shadows of shadows, yet unlike themselves,
Behind them; some like eaglets on the wing

'Were lost in the white day; others like elves
Danced in a thousand unimagined shapes
Upon the sunny streams and grassy shelves;

'And others sate chattering like restless apes
On vulgar hands, . . .
Some made a cradle of the ermined capes

'Of kingly mantles; some across the tiar
Of pontiffs sate like vultures; others played
Under the crown which girt with empire

'A baby's or an idiot's brow, and made
Their nests in it. The old anatomies
Sate hatching their bare broods under the shade

'Of daemon wings, and laughed from their dead eyes
To reassume the delegated power,
Arrayed in which those worms did monarchize,

'Who made this earth their charnel. Others more
Humble, like falcons, sate upon the fist
Of common men, and round their heads did soar;

'Or like small gnats and flies, as thick as mist
On evening marshes, thronged about the brow
Of lawyers, statesmen, priest and theorist; –

'And others, like discoloured flakes of snow
On fairest bosoms and the sunniest hair,
Fell, and were melted by the youthful glow

'Which they extinguished; and, like tears, they were
A veil to those from whose faint lids they rained
In drops of sorrow. I became aware

'Of whence those forms proceeded which thus stained
The track in which we moved. After brief space,
From every form the beauty slowly waned;

'From every firmest limb and fairest face
The strength and freshness fell like dust, and left
The action and the shape without the grace

'Of life. The marble brow of youth was cleft
With care; and in those eyes where once hope shone,
Desire, like a lioness bereft

'Of her last cub, glared ere it died; each one
Of that great crowd sent forth incessantly
These shadows, numerous as the dead leaves blown

'In autumn evening from a poplar tree.
Each like himself and like each other were
At first; but some distorted seemed to be

'Obscure clouds, moulded by the casual air;
And of this stuff the car's creative ray
Wrought all the busy phantoms that were there,

'As the sun shapes the clouds; thus on the way
Mask after mask fell from the countenance
And form of all; and long before the day

'Was old, the joy which waked like heaven's glance
The sleepers in the oblivious valley, died;
And some grew weary of the ghastly dance,

'And fell, as I have fallen, by the wayside; –
Those soonest from whose forms most shadows passed,
And least of strength and beauty did abide.

'Then, what is life? I cried.' –

INDEX OF FIRST LINES